Culture
Redefined

Thanks for All Your Support Adi

Culture Redefined

A Leadership Strategy Towards Stakeholder Capitalism:
A Time for Change

James Bailey

Published in 2021

Copyright © 2021 by James Bailey

info@omega-solutions.co.uk

ISBN, paperback: 978-1-80227-160-7
ISBN, ebook: 978-1-80227-161-4

This book is typeset in Avenir Next

Contents

Foreword

"WAVE Refrigeration have been a part of the Investors in People community since late 2019 and it always fills me with pride to see an organisation come on leaps and bounds by putting their people at the heart of everything they do. It's clear that James has done just that at WAVE, attributed by their already remarkable benchmark scores going up and up! We are delighted to have WAVE as part of our community. This book highlights exactly what a great leader looks like, the challenges they must overcome, the questions they must ask themselves and what a great company looks like too. Many congratulations to James on what I am sure will be a remarkable success, just like WAVE, as well as a useful tool to many current and aspiring leaders".

- Paul Devoy CEO of Investors in People

Culture Redefined

The Aims and Objectives of Culture Redefined

Culture Redefined conveys an evolving case study based on my experience of starting a business, growing, leading and transitioning to an employee-owned business model. The book also blends practical experience and personal reflections through the application of management theory. Culture is at the heart of my work. It is, and will always be, my key strategic driver in business, with my experiences and beliefs shared in this book.

As I have an interest in horology, the twelve chapters represent hourly goals that move towards twelve o'clock. Each hourly chapter focuses on a specific theme, from establishing a business concept to delivering sustainable, ethical and repeatable success. The overriding goal of Culture Redefined is to promote a leadership strategy that works towards the progressive ideals of stakeholder capitalism as a concept that will help organisations survive and thrive during a time of change.

Employee ownership is an operating model that is central to this book. It is a concept shift, away from traditional shareholder structures to a focus on creating lasting, resilient, people-orientated and sustainable businesses, where employees play a part in decision making and direction.

The target audience of Culture Redefined are: those who are interested in the principles of stakeholder capitalism, including experienced management professionals and business owners; people with limited management experience but who have a grounding in business management theory; students who have an interest in business and management; and people interested in exploring employee ownership as a fair and equitable business operating model.

My academic background has provided me with a 'toolbox of solutions' that I rely on in equal measure alongside my practical experience. Both have been instrumental in achieving success in the world of small business. The narrative style of Culture Redefined is one of informing, reinforming and reinforcing, supporting the reader in gaining knowledge transfer. This is a learning style that has taught me to learn, reflect and implement successful change as a business leader.

Prologue

I established WAVE Refrigeration, a company that provides professional engineering services to food retailers, in November 2015. My original intent was to provide specialist consultancy services on a small scale to refrigeration industry companies that required additional technical and project support.

As with many start-ups, during the first eighteen months of trading, I worked long hours almost daily as the need for our services grew. All the time, I was being supported by my wife, Joanne. Balancing work commitments with family life was difficult, but my passion for delivering my mission and vision remained steadfast. Through a blend of hard work, determination to succeed, and good fortune, we were appointed as ASDA's refrigeration consultant in late 2016 – this was a significant catalyst for our growth. In 2017, as we grew, we were successfully awarded a refrigeration professional services contract with ALDI, which marked the real arrival of the business, and we started gaining industry attention and respect.

As we continued to grow, gaining further retail customers, I was joined by colleagues who had significant industry experience and, importantly, who shared in my mission and vision. I set about creating a culture of excellence. My focus has never been on a defined growth strategy; it is about the creation of the very best, people-centric culture. As long as you understand the industry that you operate in, have a clear mission and vision alongside ethical beliefs and values and have products or services that customers need, allow your culture to do the rest. Empower your people and, most importantly, trust them!

Though not to everyone's taste, I am passionate about marketing and PR. I make no apology for sharing our success via social media - it is free and provides positive publicity that reaches thousands of people. Plus, most importantly, it keeps the business at the forefront of the industry. The team at WAVE share my ethos when it comes to marketing and publicity. We have won local and national awards for our work. Publicity has helped attract blue-chip clients, enhancing our culture, and most importantly, it keeps our team in well-paid and enjoyable jobs with a company that cares about their people, customers and the environment in equal measure.

Before establishing my own company, I had the good fortune to work for some exceptional people, all of whom had different ways of leading a team. I adopted what I considered to be the best characteristics of transformational leadership from my previous employers, alongside my academic learnings, but centralised organisational culture as my key driver to ensure success. Through a blend of decisiveness, promoting and encouraging individual accountability, the culture at WAVE is industry-leading.

To combat an ageing engineering industry, I set about creating a next generation programme by annually recruiting a trainee to the business. The decision to do so has reaped immeasurable benefits. It has provided our young people with a career and a mindset to deliver the company mission and live by its vision, beliefs and values. I am incredibly proud of our next generation training programme. There is no greater satisfaction in overseeing the continuous development of the next generation. Two former trainees are now managers in the business who have been shortlisted for and won a number of local and national awards.

In December 2019, I led WAVE in becoming accredited as Investors in People©, where we achieved a benchmark score of 834 out of 900. We ranked seventh out of 140 Investors in People© accredited businesses who operate in the construction sector and 158th out of all 1,751 accredited businesses (0-49 employees). This demonstrated that our culture and leadership was in a healthy place. Investors in People© accreditation provided me with the catalyst for the future of what the business should be – a company that truly shared its success with its people and embraced the values of a stakeholder capitalist future. Fast forward three months, and the world as we knew it changed with devastating consequences locally, nationally and internationally due to the COVID-19 pandemic.

Following the end of the first lockdown, I began to explore a transition for my business – a 20/20 vision, to change the company into one that shares in the principles of the Great Reset – a vision of a paradigm shift towards a stakeholder capitalist future where people and the environment are placed first. On the 11th of December 2020, I delivered my 20/20 vision, and WAVE became one of less than 500 UK companies to form an Employee Ownership Trust (EOT). The basis of an EOT is a method of shared ownership whereby employees hold a controlling stake in the company in which they work via a trust. Unlike many employee-owned businesses where employees have to buy into a scheme across a small number of allocated and often lower value shares, the EOT will benefit all employees without them having to purchase shares.

The progressive ideals of an EOT have enhanced motivation, morale and the high-quality, customer-focused services that WAVE provides, which, in turn, has benefitted our customers. Due to careful historic financial management of the business, there was no external financing required as part of forming the EOT – this is something I am particularly proud of.

My belief has always been that longevity and lasting success will only occur when the very best organisational culture is at the core of any business, with its people being placed first, and where fairness and equity are the key drivers. This vision made the formation of an EOT, my 20/20 vision, a natural progression. As the business continues to grow in the future, this dynamic business model will ensure that the very best people will want to join the WAVE family. Our much-respected next generation development programme will therefore continue to thrive under the expertise of more experienced employees.

Culture Redefined shares my experiences in a holistic way, from business inception to establishing an EOT - a model that has synergy with stakeholder capitalism. As culture is at the heart of my work, my strategy is focused on the design and implementation of four equally important elements: an organisation's mission, its vision, beliefs and values, and these are conveyed throughout Culture Redefined.

Acknowledgement of Limitation

Culture Redefined conveys the experience of a professional services provider whose business model surrounds selling time. This type of model is relatively easy to manage from a perspective of projecting workload, seasonal peaks, downturns, and most importantly, managing cashflow. This is in stark contrast to companies that manufacture or sell products, whose operating models are more complex.

The relative simplicity of operating a professional services provider is a limitation that is acknowledged. However, this simplicity is not without risk. Without a product to sell, the threat of substitution is high. This risk is my first and foremost consideration, and for this reason, I will always place organisational culture as my overriding strategy in business management.

Though important for any business, it is critical for those who only sell time that its organisational culture is best-in-class to ensure that it can survive, thrive and grow. Culture Redefined provides insights into how this can be achieved through delivering customer satisfaction and ensuring that employee motivation and engagement is high.

Culture Redefined

Working Towards One o'clock
Strategy by Design

Introduction

Many people start their own business; some succeed and thrive, and others fail. Some are forced into starting their own company, whilst others do so by design. The overriding strategy of any start-up or established company should be to take away a customer's problems. Simply put, businesses should provide products or services that solve problems, layered in with a crucial aspect - the creation of a unique selling point.

The continuous delivery of a business strategy is difficult, and it is the organisation's people who will deliver it. Fulfilling a strategy is dependent on two complex entities - organisational culture and strong leadership. In designing a business strategy, and to stand a chance of success, four focal and ever-present, culture-orientated goals have to be created, implemented and adhered to at all times:

- Mission Statement
- Vision
- Beliefs
- Values

Mission Statement

A mission statement should be aspirational and showcase the aims of a company. Most start-ups will enter a competitive marketplace, unless they are fortunate enough to have invented a new, transformational product. Most new business ventures will be service-based, so it is crucial that the market sector is researched to establish a unique selling point. Irrespective of how saturated a marketplace is, there will always be an opportunity for a new, possibly more relevant, and better entrant. Established businesses should plan for this inevitability and not simply rely on historical successes and reputation. A new entrant has to be steadfast to their unique selling point, aiming to be better than the competition, focusing on quality, and ensuring that services provided present a relevant value proposition that solves problems. The mission statement that I created for WAVE was:

> *Through positive disruption, we better the norm through providing best-in-class advice, quality and value.*

A business should centralise its strategy around its mission. Entering a mature or saturated marketplace is always going to be difficult; therefore, it is essential to be a disruptor, and a mission statement should reflect this. It is absolutely necessary to excel at what the company does whilst providing high-quality services that will get the business noticed. In respect of disruption, consider this the company's unique selling point - plus a keen price point and rapid turnaround of services should be regarded as key. Creating a mission statement can be time-consuming, but the real difficulty comes from its continuous implementation. This means reliance on a business's people: its single biggest asset.

For a young company, the experience of its people is key. Recruitment should focus on tried and tested people who will deliver its mission, vision, beliefs and values, who have been there and got the T-shirt. These people have vast knowledge, relevant skills, are passionate and fleet of foot; able to react in delivering and solving problems in a time-bound manner. Once a core team has been established, it is time to focus on the future. Though an intimidating prospect, recruitment must switch to young people, known in Culture Redefined as the next generation, where extensive training and mentoring will be required.

Do not be complacent.
Irrespective of success and reputation, a company should never become complacent with its market position. There will always be those with the drive, ambition and will to succeed. Do not believe for one minute that a new entrant, no matter how small, will not succeed and overtake an organisation's position. Remain humble and always follow the company mission, vision, beliefs and values to remain successful and relevant.

Vision

A company vision should set long-term goals. In an ever-changing world, one thing remains constant – the continuous degradation of the natural environment, resources and social disparity. A business should be conscious of the impact of its activities and have a social and environmental conscience, where its people deliver the mission and live by its vision, beliefs and values. If a company's focus is simply on the bottom line, there is little point in pretending that a social and environmental conscience exists; it is greenwashing, at best, that will eventually be criticised. I defined my vision for WAVE as a company that:

> *Promotes sustainable engineering practices that protect our natural environment for present and future generations.*

Such an aspirational vision is not uncommon, though questions will arise – how is it delivered, how is it achieved, and what measurements for success are in place? It requires hard work, effort and total commitment. Achieving an aspirational, socially, and environmentally based vision will require time, resource and investment – all without a tangible return. However, the intangible benefits are immeasurable. They will include enhanced levels of teamwork, inclusive participation, the satisfaction of a job well done and, externally, recognition of what the business stands for. Delivering a vision through executing an exceptional marketing plan will provide positive publicity, recognition, plaudits and accolades.

A business should set continuous goals and initiatives aligned to its vision, where its people play a pivotal role and are involved in making the world a better place. Be under no illusion; your social and environmental goals and initiatives are not going to change the world, but do not be put off by this. It is the sum of the parts of positive change from the many that will make a difference. Everyone has a role to play to correct social injustice and improve the environment for present and future generations.

A great way for the next generation to be accountable and lead. Generally, leadership and responsibility occur over time through gaining knowledge and experience. Having a continuous plan in executing a vision based on improving the environment and social justice does not require a wealth of work/life experience. A conscience for doing the right thing is all that is needed. Let young people, the next generation, lead a team's vision-based initiatives. It instils a sense of pride, develops confidence and identifies leadership qualities.

Beliefs and Values

A strong team-based culture will ensure that strategic business objectives are achieved. This section introduces six professional, ethical and people-orientated beliefs and values that, when working in synergy, will create and ensure the very best organisational culture.

Aspirations. Serve customers and peers to the best of the organisation's ability through building and maintaining a winning team and delivering the company mission. Ensure that its work positively impacts the natural environment.

Be Better. Make the organisation's industry or sector a better place through passion, leadership and results. Ensure a team is motivated and empowered to deliver its vision. Ensure that improvements are continuous, act on feedback and be a leader who listens and learns.

Basic Beliefs. Core values that should be at the heart of a business's culture are integrity, respect, teamwork, communication, a quest for excellence, being accountable and trust. Displaying basic beliefs are executed through customer satisfaction, striving for excellence and treating everyone with respect and dignity.

People Make the Difference. Centralise a belief that a business will only succeed through the development of teamwork and empowerment of its people. Do not wield authority. Support people in both work and personal matters and share successes with them.

Place Maximum Focus on Your Customers. Be a company that is committed to helping customers succeed and aim to exceed their expectations.

Passion for Excellence. Set high expectations of the team, correct mistakes, stay optimistic and reject complacency. Recognise that excellence cannot be achieved without effective communication.

Basic Beliefs and Values.
Always focus on business aspirations. Aim to be better. Live by its basic beliefs and values, understand that people make the difference, place maximum focus on customers and always strive and be passionate in the quest for excellence. Instil the organisation's beliefs and values into its people.

Applying Schein's Three Layers of Culture to Organisational Strategy

I began studying business management principles in 2010 at Bradford College, where I became interested in the work of Schein's three layers of culture (Mullins, 2005). Schein's work instils a mindset that an organisation's structure and systems should work with culture and not against it. This is a belief that I have held centrally in creating, growing and developing an industry-leading business.

Applying Schein's Three Layers of Culture is relevant to any business. The following depicts the three key items that influence culture:

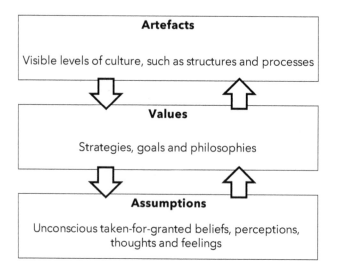

Artefacts

I set about creating a visible level and process of culture through my leadership style, which is based on a transformative approach. Whilst management may make all the significant decisions, it is important to encourage your team and make the effort to *sell* business decisions to your people. A selling approach is based on a leader who makes a decision but recognises the possibility of some resistance from those faced with the decision and subsequently persuades them to accept it.

Highly experienced remote-working employees, who you do not see on a daily basis, can unintentionally resist processes and management style. An example being the non-transference of electronic data onto a computer server. Keeping systems up to date is essential for a business's most important function – accounting and knowing when work can be invoiced. Stored electronic data is evidence of works complete, and being without it can impact on operational aims. It is necessary that an organisation's people all work together in delivering this layer of culture. Consider it like a well-oiled machine where you have the buy-in from all your people. Overlooking your artefacts can be a result of poor communication, a failure to appreciate the overall business environment and, in the example of your accounts function, can impact cash flow.

Values

Organisational values must be clearly defined. Though a business environment may be customer-focused and result-driven, designing a clear strategy that focuses on its mission, vision, beliefs, and values will ensure there is no misinterpretation of the common goals. In delivering this layer of culture, a business would be well-placed in adopting a transformational leadership position – introduced in Chapter 3. It is the role of management to instil company values in its people and ensure that they understand and buy into them. For this to happen, leaders must be visible and take a hands-on approach.

Assumptions

Taking a professional engineering services company as an example, it will likely have one customer who is accountable for a large percentage of its business sales. This can be considered as a positive, and through building and maintaining relationships while providing excellent services, there is an unconscious and often taken-for-granted belief that continuity of business and success will be achieved.

This, however, is a dangerous assumption, especially in a market where new entrants can easily penetrate a sector. An approach should rather be one of diversity and having multiple customers, ideally not representing more than 25% of your sales. In reality, this is very difficult to achieve. As a result of my experience and putting management theory into practice, my company reduced its reliance from 95% down to 60% of the business's largest customers in less than three years. This is absolutely essential for any business's longevity, as your biggest customer may see a downturn in their fortunes. If you have failed to diversify and attract more customers, which will take time, a consequence will be cutbacks in your business. Management should always look beyond current success and seek out further opportunities to ensure a lasting and secure future.

Working Towards Two o'clock
Marketing by Design

Introduction

With the exception of word-of-mouth, no one else outside of any business will promote or publicise its services. However, in today's digital world, promotion is easy. An internet search is the most likely first calling point when a customer requires a service or product. A website should be considered a shop front and be visually pleasing. Ensuring a website is up to date, relevant and easy to navigate is important. Services and products should be clearly identified and well-articulated. Where possible, include the business's people, introduce who they are and what they do. Do not feel the need to be formal or awkward, have a little fun. Your website should show potential customers the close-knit relationship of your team that exists alongside the professional services provided. Have a news section and aim to add news stories regularly, and do not be afraid to show off. Be proud and promote the business as industry pioneers and leaders. Existing customers will take satisfaction that the business is proud and shares its good news stories. After all, they have and continue to be a key to its success.

The greatest thing about the digital world for a business is that advertising or getting a story out there is instantaneous and free. Social media platforms are the single biggest source of free advertisement. Build up your contact base and use platforms like LinkedIn to share your news and successes. When posting to LinkedIn, link it to a website news post as viewers will often reroute themselves to the site, thus increasing the visibility and presence of the website and making the company a top-ranking search result. Do not be concerned with any naysayers of self-promotion. People can be envious of success, and this can bring out the worst in people! Always remember that no one else will do your advertising for you.

Invest in a partnership with a website developer.
To keep a website relevant, up to date and fresh, it is necessary to ensure that changes can be implemented with expedience. There are many website developers – choose one who wants to learn about what the business does and negotiate a monthly retainer. The output is assurance that content changes and the look and feel of a website will be carried out by someone who more than likely has excellent creative and artistic vision.

The Four Ps

The Four Ps (4Ps) marketing mix theory was popularised by Neil Borden in the 1950s. The marketing mix theory demonstrates ways that companies could use advertising strategies to attract customers. The 4Ps represent Product, Price, Place and Promotion; expanded on below.

Product

Product refers to the goods or services that a company offers, and they should fulfil and exceed customer expectations. Think unique selling point – pitch a product or service in a compelling way to create new or alternative demand. In a well-established marketplace, this will come back to the company mission where quality and value are needed, wanted and demanded by its customers.

In delivering a product or service, marketing is intrinsically connected with an organisation's culture. Where its beliefs and values are instilled throughout a team, they will not only be motivated to provide and satisfy customer demand. They will also always think beyond and provide additional value, for example, exceeding a timescale or solving further customer problems. This will ensure repeat business that allows the business to build relationships and ultimately helps it to grow and thrive.

Price

Price is the cost a customer pays for a product or service. Where a business pitches its price will be a key to its success, and it can often be considered an organisation's unique selling point. In a service-based sector, where time is being purchased, consider operational costs, seasonal downturns (where applicable), and decide on what is considered to be an appropriate mark-up and profit margin. In a market where there are multiple players, and where a company's focus is on presenting a lower-cost proposition than its competition, it is critical that the company has a well-motivated team who are prepared to go above and beyond in the sense of not keeping to strict nine-to-five type working hours.

It is highly unlikely that any organisation will have an employee who works anywhere close to 100% efficiency levels. To ensure profitability, a company will need team players who have bought into the company's mission, vision, beliefs and values and will regularly go above and beyond the call of duty to maximise efficiency. Be clear and transparent in respect to price position, and ideally offer a single pricing structure across your customer base. A key customer contact may move on to a competitor where the company also provides services - spare any form of embarrassment in having to explain different day rates.

Place

Place refers to where a product or service should be sold and delivered to the business's industry sector. Concentrating on the experience of a professional services provider, think about the geographical coverage of a team. An organisation must consider if it truly has the ability to serve customers at opposite ends of the country, for example, providing services in Land's End or John O' Groats when the majority of the team is located centrally in the UK. Whilst turning work away is not particularly palatable, there is little point in providing services that do not make commercial sense. It will tire people out whilst disrupting the services that the company provides well. Always carefully consider what a business can do well and the locations in which it can serve its customers successfully.

Place should also refer to a target customer. For example, if providing services in the retail arena, make discounters target customers. Learn from them – how they eliminate waste, how they operate lean, and so on – as it will help support business success and growth. A further example is where a business possesses high levels of ethical, societal and environmental concerns: target customers with similar beliefs and values as it is possible that they will want to work with you.

Promotion

Promotion refers to and includes advertising, public relations and promotional strategies. The goal of promoting a product or service is to showcase an organisation's ability and experience within its sector. Well-positioned marketing should target both customers and the industry. Consider a website as the company's shop window, maintain and update its content regularly and show off its people – who they are, what they do and what they have achieved. Poor website design, which is often a consequence of not understanding marketing, or because it is considered an unnecessary investment, is damaging to the brand.

Many smaller customers, whom you may never have considered targeting, will use internet searches to find a product or service. From experience, around 10% of a company's annual turnover can come from unexpected sources. Ensure that a website is relevant, easy to navigate, better than its competition, and professionalism will shine through. Unexpected customers present a two-fold positive effect. A well-informed website presents new opportunities to attract potential customers and demonstrates that a good marketing strategy works.

Do not just promote product or services. Think about the future relevance of stakeholder capitalism. Link the company vision to its marketing strategy, but do not greenwash. Businesses have a pivotal part to play in ensuring a more environmentally and socially improved future. Live by the organisation's vision and invest in it through your marketing. Though environmental and social initiatives are intangible when considering the bottom line, in a post-COVID-19 world, businesses that continue to thrive will require a societal conscience at the heart of their work.

Think the Four P way and link it with your culture.
Product - Think unique selling point. Go the extra mile to exceed customer expectations. An organisation's people are critical to achieving this. Focus your strategy on a best-in-class culture where its people go above and beyond.
Price - Add value to products or services. Understand that a business's people do not operate at a 100% efficiency level. Provide an environment that encourages motivation to add that little extra value to exceed its customers' expectations.
Place - Think where products and services will be provided. Be realistic. Target relevant customers who are growing. This will enhance job security and, in turn, have a positive impact on the organisation's culture.
Promotion - Quality of online presence is key. Use it to demonstrate the business's services, professionalism, to seek opportunity and illustrate how it lives by its vision. Include all of an organisation's people on a website and show them off to the wider world. This will significantly enhance the company culture, aspirations and goals.

Customer Satisfaction

Customer satisfaction in its meaning is a key goal of any business and, by definition, sounds simple. It is not. It must be continuous, and for this reason, a company cannot take its eye off the ball for a single second. The single biggest factor in ensuring customer satisfaction is its people. This is why the design of an overriding culture-orientated, people-focused strategy is crucial. Teamwork, individual autonomy and responsibility, the operating environment, motivation, and management having the ability to listen and learn from mistakes will set the tone of a business's culture. To ensure that an organisation's culture is successful, management must be approachable and provide motivation to the business's people, ensuring that they do not live in fear of making mistakes. They should instil confidence and establish an environment that allows mistakes to be openly discussed and corrected.

When it comes to achieving customer satisfaction, management must constantly communicate with their team, be challenging, provide opportunities for them to improve ways of working, listen to them and learn from them. If a company has an excellent culture (though it can always be better), e.g., the team delivers its mission, live by the vision, and have totally bought into its beliefs and values, a company stands a fighting chance in ensuring customer satisfaction. A team cannot be solely accountable for this. Management must be visible, involved and get stuck into delivering products and services. In doing so, they will keep an eye on the ball and improve the chances of retaining business, whilst the organisation continues to grow and thrive.

Customer feedback should be sought when a company is busy and all of its people are in the trenches. Seeking out ways in which performance can be improved is a great way to hear the voice of the customer. Though a business may provide an excellent product or service, perfection will never be achieved. However, this does not mean that it should not be an aspiration or that good is good enough. Listen attentively to customers and act on feedback, no matter how small. Customers will be confident that a supplier is prepared to introduce processes to enhance their experience based on communication with them - it demonstrates that the customer comes first and that seeking feedback is a conversation worth having. Management must work with and involve their team to ensure that customer feedback is acted on and a greater level of satisfaction is received. Inclusivity in the decision-making processes of improving customer satisfaction is key. Again, highlighting just how important culture is, it must be considered a continuous and evolving journey.

Ensuring satisfaction.
A culture-inspired strategy relies on a business delivering its mission, living by its vision, cementing its beliefs and values, and empowering its people. They should set the tone in ensuring customer satisfaction. Management need to be visible, seek feedback and improvements, implement change to enhance customer experience, and involve all of an organisation's people to deliver ever-increasing levels of satisfaction.

Relationships

Building lasting relationships is key to a successful business, and it is assumed that through positive organisational culture, an organisation's management will have a good relationship with their people. Externally, relationships should not just extend to its customers. Seek to build, maintain and enhance relationships with industry peers, as this will help to seek out business opportunities. Maintaining a healthy relationship with competitors is not a bad thing. Regular communication through cooperation, as opposed to competition, can actually encourage innovation. A business's competitors should not be considered a rival that cannot be engaged, though there should be an aspiration to be better. Competitors have the same objective in respect of providing an excellent service and keeping people employed. Building and maintaining relationships can be easy, or it can be difficult. Everyone is different. A leader can be an introvert or extrovert by nature, just as a business's customers and industry peers will be too. Seeking and finding common ground is important, though the overriding theme from all stakeholders will be getting the job done.

In a customer-facing business, everyone has a role to play. Though it should be headed up by an organisation's people, it should be backed up by management. The key is to be positive, energetic and engaging, and considered as someone who gets the job done. Building professional working relationships should not be considered a popularity contest or a means to seek approval. The very best relationships are based on achieving common and wider objectives.

An important consideration is etiquette and how a business presents itself. Some customers will be highly driven, motivated, career-focused, with a real flare, and possess fantastic corporate attributes that will take them to the top of their own organisation. Above all, when interacting with customers, be yourself, talk with passion and enthusiasm. Be seen as someone who leads by example and gets the job done.

Build relationships that last.
It costs nothing to communicate, and effective communication will foster long-term relationships. Establish common ground and talk with passion and enthusiasm. Showcase that the business gets the job done and provides constant support to its customers. They may take your organisation on their career journey, which could be highly rewarding to a business's future success and growth. Demonstrating hard work, having the ability to build lasting relationships, and networking are all key to building and maintaining an organisation's brand reputation.

Applying Porter's Five Forces to Marketing Strategy

A measure of an organisation's success will be how well you understand your operating environment and your ability to react and adapt to change. Since being introduced to Michael E. Porter's *Five Forces* (Mintzberg, 1992), I have used and applied the concept countless times, and it is now part of my subconscious thought process.

As a concept, Porter's Five Forces are simple to understand, and if applied to the context of a business's marketing strategy, they will prove invaluable. It is an ideal model to analyse competitive forces as they will determine your operating environment and your company's profit potential. Though I have never been driven by profit or, more specifically, achieving a set margin, to be successful and allow a business to grow, profit is essential. It is how profit or wealth is distributed that is a concern to me. The following model depicts how I apply Porter's Five Forces in marketing.

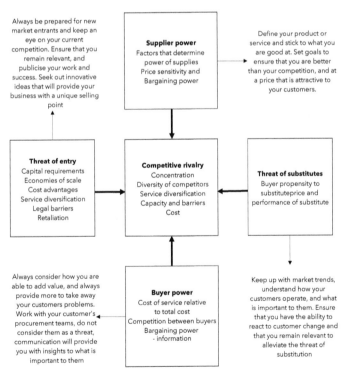

From my experience, the most important consideration from Porter's Five Forces surrounds the value that businesses should seek to add to their customers. Providing value to the products or services that you provide will help form long-lasting relationships. The model also helps a business retain focus when it comes to understanding its operating environment, e.g., who its competitors are, who could be considered as its substitutes, and how a business can improve the way it publicises its products or services. Having a deep and thorough understanding of a company's operating environment is essential to thrive, survive and most importantly, as explored in Chapter 3, business growth.

Working Towards Three o'clock
Growth

Introduction

Having an idea about setting up a business by choice or through necessity is an exciting time, but nothing can prepare you for the realities and hard work that is required. Basic advice includes creating a business plan, goal setting, and revisiting and updating a plan regularly. In the beginning, it is important to accept and be prepared for long days, setbacks and frustrations. To set the foundations of a successful business, it is necessary to make sacrifices. Dedication and setting personal goals will help ensure that support is provided by family and friends. Having to cope with unexpected setbacks and the management of finances must be careful considerations. Seek to be surrounded by positive and motivational people.

Having a sound business model and a well-designed strategy will help a new company to succeed, but in those early days, its founder must be prepared to do everything themselves. From providing all services and products to creating standard documents, raising invoices and managing cash flow: working days will be long and tiring. Use the early days to think about partners: specifically, accountancy and IT support. Consider what the business is going to be, e.g., size, customer base, core services, principles, why it is different from its competitors, the type of people it will require, and how lean the business can be. Also, bear in mind those critical operational roles such as office management and administration support that are often underestimated by businesses. When workload is such that critical mass is reached, and when cash flow allows, embrace the investment associated with growth opportunities. Though daunting, this mindset, alongside remaining positive, is critical in achieving successful growth.

Have an eye on the future.
Perseverance and determination to succeed through sacrifice will reap the rewards and set the company up for a successful future. Upon critical mass, have the confidence to invest as the business embarks on its journey of growth.

Transformational Leadership

In a mature market where there are already multiple players, strong and focused business leadership is critical to achieving growth. When striving for the very best culture in an organisation, management will be well placed to adopt transformational traits. Take control by conveying a clear vision of the company goals, show passion for all work, and have the energy to make the growing team feel motivated. Transformational leadership inspires positive changes in those who follow. Management need to have an interest in and be involved in all of a business's activities, plus be focused on helping all of its people succeed.

For transformational leadership to occur and succeed, it depends principally on the design of the business's strategy. Create a clear and instilled mission, an environmentally and socially just vision, working in conjunction with shared beliefs and values. Transformational leadership will be recognised externally, too; the organisation's industry will respect and admire what it is achieving. This respect and admiration will increase further through being seen as pioneers in addressing social injustices and playing a part to improve our natural environment.

Changing attitudes and the wider introduction of progressive stakeholder capitalist beliefs and values will continue to gain momentum in a post-COVID-19 world. As global beliefs and values change, be a leader who is not only prepared but also passionate about playing a part in the Great Reset (discussed in later chapters).

The concept of transformational leadership was introduced by James V. Downton and was further developed by James MacGregor Burns (2004). Burns suggested that transformational leadership can be defined based on the impact that it has on its followers – an organisation's people and industry peers. Researcher Bernard M. Bass expanded upon Burns' original ideas and suggested that there are four components of transformational leadership:

Intellectual Stimulation: Transformational leaders are those who challenge the status quo and shift traditional paradigms. They encourage creativity among their people and peers. They spur them on to explore new ways of working and create opportunities for them to learn.

Individualised Consideration: Transformational leaders support and provide encouragement to individuals. To promote and deliver supportive relationships, they keep lines of communication open so that their people feel able to discuss and share their ideas.

Inspirational Motivation: Transformational leaders strictly follow and adhere to their mission, vision, beliefs and values at all times. They are able to articulate the organisation's goals to its people. Transformational leaders also help their people work towards the same level of passion and motivation to fulfil organisational goals.

Idealised Influence: Transformational leaders serve as role models to their people. Where an organisation's people trust and respect their leaders, they will emulate their ideals.

Transformational leadership is highly effective, but it might not be the best choice for every situation. In some cases, individuals or teams may require a traditional managerial or autocratic style that involves closer control and greater direction, particularly when working with less experienced team members.

Know your mission, vision, beliefs and values inside out.
To be a transformational leader, you have to undertake, instil, deliver
and live by the company's mission, vision, beliefs and values every
single day. Be passionate, energetic, inspirational and motivational
to the organisation's people, and be prepared to embrace change,
pursue ideas and continually seek to be better.

Applying Leadership Theory to Support Business Growth

An organisation's culture is the single biggest factor in achieving and
maintaining strategy as a business grows, where the aim is to meet
and exceed customer requirements. It is essential that its people have
bought into and deliver the company mission, living by its vision,
beliefs and values.

Sharing my experiences regarding your culture as the foundation
of achieving and maintaining a successful business strategy comes
down to leadership style. The toolbox of theoretical management
solutions that I have applied in leading my team has been in the form
of transformational leadership. This style is focused on engendering
motivation and commitment, which creates a vision for transforming
the organisation's performance and appeals to the higher ideals and
values of an organisation's people.

Whilst perfection will never be realised, a culture that drives
leadership to focus on continuous improvement will support the
delivery of a transformational environment with a far-reaching goal
of being perfect.

As a business grows, there should be a purpose to wider
organisational goals. From my experience, I drew upon five
philosophies, and how I interpreted these are summarised below:

- Challenge - Having a long-term vision of challenges that
  an organisation faces is critical to realising your ambition in
  achieving goals.

- Kaizen - No process can ever be considered perfect, so operations must be improved continuously, ensuring innovation and evolution.
- Genchi Genbutsu – Leadership goes to the source of the issue to see the facts, make the right decisions, create consensus and ensure objectives are achieved.
- Respect - Taking all employees' problems seriously, building trust and taking responsibility for other people reaching their objectives.
- Teamwork - Developing individuals through problem-solving, creating ideas and valued contribution.

In a leadership context, it is possible to gain the following insights into the theory of transformational leadership through the creation of:

- a feeling of justice within the team.
- instilling loyalty within the team.
- instilling trust in both a leader and the team.

In summary, transformational leadership in an organisational sense is concerned with the performance of a business. This type of leadership is effective where continuous improvement of results is necessary. By employing principles of continuous improvement and being able to include and motivate all of an organisation's people, transformational leadership will be successful and ensure an organisation maintains and exceeds its aspirations and goals.

Though I am a huge advocate of transformational leadership, it is important to consider other leadership styles and demonstrate why being a participative and transformational leader is the most effective style in today's changing world. In his book *Management and Organisational Behaviours*, Laurie Mullins (2005) describes leadership as, "The way in which the functions of leadership are carried out, the way in which the manager typically behaves towards members of the group." Although there are many possible ways of describing leadership styles, for example, dictatorial, unitary, bureaucratic, benevolent, charismatic, consultative, and participative, Mullins suggests that style can be classified within a broad three-fold heading: autocratic, democratic/participative, and laissez-faire/free-rein.

The college of St. Scholastica reported on the 1938 study *Leadership and Group Life*, conducted by Lewin et al. This study introduced these same three broad styles of leadership. The result found that the democratic/participative style was superior to either the autocratic or laissez-faire styles.

Supporting this theory and cited by Mullins is Blake and Mouton (2005), who suggested that, "An organisation is more likely to harness its staffing resources effectively if there is a participative style of management." The following model depicts a representation of the Blake and Mouton Leadership Grid®.

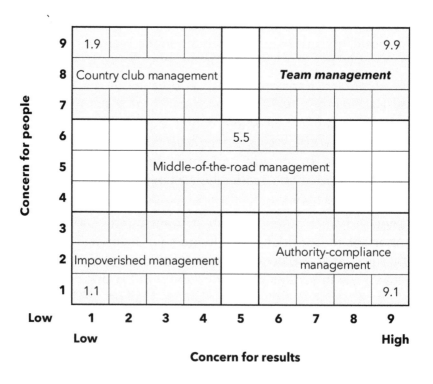

Blake and Moulton, though defining the best leadership as 'team management', has parallels with transformational leadership. The work of Blake and Moulton can be contrasted with the work of Lewin et al. The following model is an interpretation where the classification of the three broad styles of leadership is compared with the leadership grid from my personal experience.

Blake & Moulton - Leadership type	Definition	Lewin - Broad style category
9.1 Authority-compliance management	Leaders in this position have great concern for results but not for people.	Autocratic
1.9 Country club management	Leaders in this position have great concern for people but little concern for results.	
1.1 Impoverished management	Leaders in this position have little concern for either results or people.	Laissez-faire
5.5 Middle-of-the-road management	Leaders in this position have medium concern for both results and people.	
9.9 Team management	Leaders demonstrate high concern for both results and people. They work to motivate employees; they are considered flexible and responsive; they are **transformational.**	Participative

Even in the earlier part of the twentieth century, it was clear that an inclusive, participative or, in today's context, a transformational leadership style was superior. It is currently preferred if a business specifically seeks to grow and maintain the very best organisational culture, where people and results are of equal importance.

Culture Redefined

Working Towards Four o'clock
The Next Generation

Introduction

In establishing a successful business, management will be surrounded by experienced professionals who are tried and tested and have a track record of delivering results. Irrespective of the industry, the business's leaders will have known the people personally, or the type of individual will have been identified by the business. These people will be those who will deliver the organisation's mission and live by the vision, beliefs and values. Eventually, an organisation will reach a stage in its growth that poses the question: who should be recruited next? All businesses need people who will fit seamlessly into the organisation's culture, and management may have exhausted those 'natural fit' people they would like to join the business.

Company management will undoubtedly know many talented professionals who could work for the business, but will they fit into the culture - the most important component in delivering its strategy? If the answer is no, as it may inevitably be, recruitment should take a different path. Though in some respects a daunting prospect, to ensure the survival of the established organisational culture, the company will have to build and mould its own people. This will lead them to the next generation: graduates and school leavers who have very little in the way of experience.

There is a lot of scepticism surrounding Generation Z (categorised as being born between the mid-to-late 1990s and early 2010s).

However, a business should not be put off by this in its recruitment plans. The reality is that this generation is desperate for an opportunity and to be given a chance. As long as a company recruits carefully, it will be repaid in the form of the most committed, loyal and hardworking people who make exceptional team players.

The next generation are not going to hit the ground running, and an organisation needs to be prepared for this. Management will also need to rely on its experienced people who will play a significant part in training and developing the next generation. Mentoring, patience, enthusiasm and energy will be key to the success that the business enjoys from the next generation. For a business owner and leader, there is no prouder feeling than seeing young people succeed. There is no greater satisfaction than seeing future leaders grow in confidence, gain experience, take on responsibility, be accountable and play their part in the business's success.

Embrace the next generation.
Young people starting out in their careers need an opportunity, and if a business recruits well, it will be rewarded beyond its expectations. Though it is important to recruit academically gifted talent, do not solely focus on the brightest. As long as young people are willing to learn, work hard and have a spark, take a chance on them and embrace what they can bring to the business. In a very short period of time, they will be valuable members of the team who contribute to its success.

Increasing Capacity through Development

Unlocking the potential of young and inexperienced people is key to increasing capacity as an organisation grows. There are two important focus areas that need to be considered when unlocking potential: giving sufficient time to mentor them and trusting them to deliver with limited experience. A business and its leadership must be prepared for mistakes as they will occur. However, having designed a strategy around its culture allows for errors to be corrected and lessons to be learned. Making mistakes and learning from those made are at the core of delivering rapid development. Working in synergy with a business's culture provides the next generation with the enthusiasm to want to be better and enjoy the steep learning trajectory they have embarked on.

When it comes to the next generation, the traditional method of learning on the job and receiving annual salary increments is not necessarily sufficient if seeking rapid development. Management should seek out ways to take motivation to the next level. From experience, these include:

- Twice-yearly appraisals where goals are set and agreed upon, and work is provided to focus young people on attaining them.
- Consistent and continuous communication – be visible and approachable, encourage and provide feedback, good or bad, on a regular basis.
- Seek out opportunities for young people and showcase what they have done. A good way to do this is by entering them into awards and events that recognise young talent. Winning an award is fantastic, but even being shortlisted will instil a sense of pride and enhance their motivation. Recognition of young people also provides publicity and a positive reflection of the business.
- Let the next generation lead a company's vision-based initiatives. This instils a sense of pride, develops confidence and identifies leadership qualities. In doing so, the scene is being set early for continuous succession planning in the business.

Mentoring and developing the next generation cannot be considered in isolation for one person. It will rely on the support of everyone in the company, and this will be driven by how good and effective its organisational culture is. The resultant output will be a greater number of skilled people who have been moulded into the expected norms and ways of working, ultimately allowing the business to continuously grow and thrive.

The next generation is key in preparing a business for longevity. Unlocking the potential of the next generation with expedience is key to supporting and preparing a business for growth. Be prepared to invest significant amounts of time in young people. Constantly communicate and give feedback. Do not sugar-coat any areas where improvement is required in their performance. Be direct, as this will help prepare them for senior roles within the business. Showcase your business's young talent. Not only will they feel proud and be motivated, but it will also reflect positively on the business and demonstrate that you walk the walk and talk the talk in implementing an industry-leading culture.

A Loyal and Talented Workforce

On joining a business, young people will have very little in the way of experience and will possibly be low on confidence. It is not only the role of company leadership, but everyone in the business, to welcome, embrace, nurture and train the next generation. This will only occur through the design of a business's strategy and its steadfast implementation that revolves around its organisational culture. An impactful way to push the next generation is to provide direct client exposure at an early stage within a business. Alongside gaining knowledge, young people will feel totally involved and understand the importance of the role that they have to play.

Young people will constantly absorb and process information and will continuously gain invaluable experience. As long as sufficient time is invested, along with direct mentoring from the top of an organisation, they will rapidly flourish, learn, consistently improve, seek out responsibility and carve out a role for themselves.

The output of a young person who has been provided with a career opportunity will have synergy with their peers who have experience, and the organisation will be rewarded with the most loyal and talented workforce.

To be better, to thrive and to grow a business requires a top-down commitment from every single person within an organisation. A relatively invisible or unconsidered benefit of developing the next generation is the sense of pride your experienced people will feel having played their part in developing talent that is ready to contribute right now and more so in the future. Management should recognise the importance of acknowledging the efforts of its more experienced team members for helping in the development of the next generation. Their time and effort should not be overlooked. Delivering an organisation's mission, living its vision and believing in its beliefs and values will ensure that acknowledging all of a team becomes second nature to management. If there is any doubt in the minds of a business's management team, the design of its culture-based strategy may need reassessing.

Total commitment is key.
Total commitment is required to benefit from a loyal and talented workforce, extending not only to the next generation but to the whole team. If management are not fully committed to unlocking the potential of millennial talent, do not waste time or effort. If, however, the business does have an eye on the future and growth, and management has designed its strategy around organisational culture, embrace the opportunity that young people present to a business. They are an additional expense, and they will consume an infinite amount of time, but the business will be repaid through loyalty and the thirst to learn in their quest to becoming a talented member of a team. This will also play an important part in an organisation's growth aspirations.

Applying Theory to Support the Development of the Next Generation

A measure of success in developing the next generation is through minimal or no resistance from either a business's trainees or its experienced people. In the work and model of Kotter and Schlesinger (1979), they proposed an emergent approach to tackling employee resistance. I have applied each of their five proposed approaches as a continuous growth strategy connected with the development of the next generation, ensuring success rather than resistance. Each approach describes when they should be used in the context of developing the next generation, and the advantages and drawbacks of all approaches are identified in the following model:

Approach	Commonly used in these situations	How the approach relates to the development of the next generation	Advantages	Drawbacks
Education & communication	Lack of information or inaccurate information	Management must lead in regular communication, conveying information and the mentoring of the next generation, but all members of a team have a part to play in their development	Inclusive participation through sharing of knowledge and information from all members of a team who will be rewarded in the development of the next generation: this supports growth	Mentoring can be time-consuming, without immediate rewards
Participation & involvement	Initiators of change do not have all the information to implement change and there is potential to resist	Each young team member will have different skills and learn at a different pace. It is important that the imparting of information and knowledge through mentoring is appropriate, based on an individuals needs - this is to prevent resistance	Each young team member will gain a sense of specific care towards them by taking a non-generic approach to their development	People learn and develop at a different pace. It is important to consider this to ensure that there are not unrealistic expectations
Facilitation & support	Where employees resist due to adjustment issues	This relates to taking a young team member out of a familiar environment and setting them a challenge. Though they must be mentored and guided, this does not mean that they shouldn't be stretched and challenged	Being 'thrown into the deep end' has significant benefits - learning, experience & knowledge is gained rapidly	Without support when challenging the next generation, there is a risk of causing upset and demotivation

Negotiation & agreement	Someone or some group will lose out in change and they have considerable power to resist change	This relates to the necessity of regular appraisals where goals and targets are set. It is important to be challenging and clear to young people to allow them to have visibility of the business's expectations in terms of their growth and ability to change	Appraisals and reviews, in tandem with regular communication, will clearly set objectives for its young people to aspire to and attain	Young people may not have the confidence to challenge what they consider is a difficult objective to achieve. A good appraisal process and regular communication is key
Manipulation & co-operation	Where other tactics will not work, or are too expensive	This relates to experienced team members who may not have bought in to the development of the next generation through their own fears. It is therefore important within a best-in-class culture business to provide feedback and praise to all team members involved in mentoring and training, to acknowledge their efforts	A whole business and its people are rewarded and gain satisfaction in seeing the next generation develop and thrive	In not acknowledging the efforts of all those involved in training and mentoring, there is a risk of individual job security fears and feelings of being left out

Though classically linked as a theory to overcome direct resistance, I have found that Kotter and Schlesinger's approaches are ideally placed to set strategies related to unlocking the potential of the next generation. All approaches can be considered as critical elements in the successful development of next generation talent as they learn and develop in a business. The five approaches have the added benefit of identifying and addressing any possible resistance. This ensures that the next generation works in harmony with an organisation's experienced people and ultimately with the organisation's culture.

Next generation talent will always be influenced by the behaviours of their managers and colleagues. For this reason, it is necessary that the design of your strategy is influenced and revolves around your culture. With respect to culture, Charles Handy (1985) proposed that there are four types: Power, Role, Task and Person.

The following model identifies and interprets each of the four types of culture identified by Handy:

Power Culture	Role Culture
Control radiates from the centre - people are encouraged to have absolute belief in its leaders. Power is concentrated among senior management. There are little in the way of rules, or red tape. People are encouraged to deliver the company mission, and live its vision, beliefs and values. Decision making is swift - allowing all people to be fleet of foot and work at pace.	People have designated levels of authority. The structure follows a hierarchy and can be considered bureaucratic. Power is derived from the position held by individual. Little in the way of scope exists for expert power.
Task Culture	**People Culture**
Teams are formed to solve problems. Power is derived from expertise. There is no single power source. There is overlap between people and departments.	People can consider themselves superior to the business. Common in professional service organisations. People have similar training, backgrounds and experience. Power is with particular groups of individuals.

From my experience of establishing and building a successful business that focuses on being a disruptor within its sector, I centralised Handy's four types of culture on Power. Over time, as the team gelled together, Task culture has found its place and is now as important as Power culture. For both experienced employees and the next generation, Task culture is highly important if considering a transition to a stakeholder capitalist business operating model such as employee ownership. Handy's four types of culture model is revisited in Chapter 12.

Power culture for a small yet formidable business is highly desirable, especially in the early days of growth and securing and solidifying its market position. From my experience as a professional services provider, this could be considered controversial or even contradictory, as People culture could be considered the natural fit, but, in my experience, it is neither! Unfortunately, some people can believe that they are superior to a business and its mission, vision, beliefs and values. No matter how talented people are, if they place their own needs and, in some instances, their agenda above those of the business, then it is time to move forward without them. Your young people, the next generation, could become influenced by those people who consider themselves beyond reproach. For an employee-owned business, in particular, People culture must be avoided – there is no 'I' in a successful team.

Culture Redefined

Working Towards Five o'clock
Reward Management

Introduction

Workplace reward is an integral aspect of a business's success. A key component of a strategy that is designed around a best-in-class culture is reward management. This is central to employee productivity, which in turn is connected to the overall profitability and survival of any business.

In today's changing world, it is no longer viable to believe that a strategy based on the delivery of an organisation's goals can occur without involving workplace reward. Reward management should be considered as a source of gaining a sustained competitive advantage for a business. Outdated paradigms that focus solely on a competitive pay structure to ensure the delivery of a company's goals are not sufficient to guarantee productivity, profitability, or survival.

Since the late noughties, economies and people have had to endure difficult periods. The credit crunch and subsequent recession that began in 2008, the increase in university tuition fees, the ongoing and worsening concern of climate change, and more recently, the COVID-19 pandemic are all ingredients that have changed people's attitudes. Change in attitude has not been borne out of greed; it is a change borne out of necessity, as people seek ways to improve their own security in both their work and personal lives.

Change in attitudes that relate to the workplace does not extend to any single particular age profile. At one end of the spectrum, there are experienced people who are seeking security to ensure they remain employed until they retire. Then, at the other end of the spectrum, there are those starting their careers who are concerned about the repayment of tuition fees whilst, at the same time, attempting to get ahead in life. The two common themes that connect all age profiles regarding a change in attitudes is a drive to build a stronger, more secure economy, and address climate change. These themes were the key driver in implementing a continuous, beyond-the-bottom-line programme and initiative, to be introduced in Chapter 6.

The link between reward management and changing attitudes. Economic and climatic events since the late noughties have changed people's attitudes. It is now crucially important for businesses to think beyond traditional reward mechanisms that are only linked to pay. Long-lasting financial security and being seen to contribute actively to ameliorating climate change are key ingredients in reward management and are directly linked to the aims of stakeholder capitalism.

Motivation

Linking changing attitudes with reward management is critical in achieving business goals of productivity, profitability and survival. The companies that will thrive in the post-COVID-19 future are prepared to adapt to change and genuinely seek to implement the very best organisational culture. Changing attitudes should not be feared by businesses and their leaders; they should be embraced.

The first part of this chapter explores eight directly linked effective and transformative leadership traits that are central to successful employee motivation.

1. Trust People.

To ensure the continuity and longevity of any organisation, it is important that its employees know they are trusted. In demonstrating trust, future leaders will shine through, and they will be ready for additional responsibility in the knowledge that they can make mistakes as long as they are corrected.

Trust will also ensure that a business's people work to the best of their ability to deliver the business's goals and will rarely disappoint.

2. Give People Purpose.

Give an organisation's people purpose. In accomplishing this, they will fully understand the mission, vision, beliefs and values that work together to achieve the overriding goals of the company.

By understanding their purpose and the business's purpose, its people can better understand how they fit into the big picture and the positive difference that they can make.

3. Be Positive.

'Getting the job done' is always going to be an overriding aim of any business. An organisation's people will gain motivation through the energy, enthusiasm and traits that management display. In 'getting the job done' well, you instil positivity into the workplace. During the working day make time to talk and have breaks together where people feel able to talk about non-work-related topics.

The positivity transmitted from the top will cultivate a relaxed environment that ensures the delivery of results.

4. Be Transparent.

Be open with employees about what is happening at the highest level – this will ensure that there are no surprises and that everyone has a chance to ask questions, give feedback and participate. Management should seek to make people feel that they are included in big decisions. They will then be motivated and committed to the direction that the company takes.

Being transparent will help sustain and enhance motivation whilst increasing loyalty and pride.

5. Have an Open-Door Policy.

Though simple in nature, saying please and thank you costs nothing, but it shows respect and will resonate with an organisation's people. When management are polite, it promotes an open-door policy, and the resultant effect can be employees become more likely to suggest ideas and improvements to make the business better.

When employees feel that their voice matters, they feel confident about their position and role in an organisation.

6. Let People Lead

Motivating people is not limited to good pay and conditions; it is about showing them that they make a difference and are valued. Every time a company has a meeting, whether large or small, its people should be allowed to lead the conversation based on topic.

Even the next generation can lead conversations and the topics discussed. Not only will people share their opinions and be heard, but they are motivated to make their words and ideas happen afterwards.

7. Show People the Bigger Picture.

It is important that a business's people understand the bigger picture and can see that what they are doing at the moment will eventually contribute to an end goal.

Allocate tasks and projects to work on that shows them how they fit into the big picture. This will keep motivation levels high.

8. Recognise and Praise a Job Well Done.

At every internal team meeting, recognise people who have done a great job or have gone above and beyond. Keep track of the recognition provided. This will allow management to focus on ensuring that everyone regularly earns praise in front of their colleagues.

Recognition and praise should be a cornerstone of transformational leadership and considered as a continuous feedback loop to motivate people, as depicted in the following model:

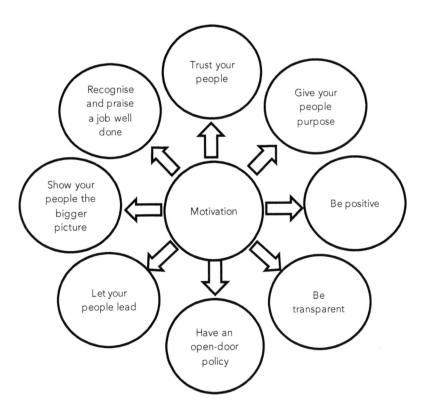

Reward on Circumstance – Everyone is Different

Transformational leadership and motivation are the key ingredients to successful reward management. It is important to recognise that individual rewards will be circumstance based: all of an organisation's people will have different wants and needs.

Designing a strategy to motivate in multiple ways based on circumstance ensures each stakeholder has a clear, personal understanding of how working together benefits themselves and the team. Listen and learn about the aspirations of the employees of the business. The next generation are likely to want to expand their knowledge base and gain recognised qualifications in their area of expertise. Subconsciously, they will feel that qualifications will provide them with the security of finding alternative employment if there is a decline and downturn in business. From a management perspective, this subconscious thought process should have no bearing whatsoever. A business strategy centred around its culture will ensure that the next generation bring their skills acquired from qualifications into the workplace, and this, in turn, will benefit the company.

People who have a wealth of experience will not be as likely to want to gain further qualifications; however, they will want the business to tap into their wealth of knowledge. Management should focus on specific areas of expertise and knowledge that experienced people bring to the business. Provide them with time, resources and autonomy to implement ideas that will benefit the business based on their experience and skill set. Rewarding people based on individual circumstances, such as providing learning and development opportunities, or tapping into the knowledge of experienced employees, allows a business to motivate all of its people to accomplish and surpass the company's goals.

Throughout a team, management should ask, listen and learn about what its people like doing and what they do not like doing. Share the company's goals and respond to their questions. Discover what their professional and personal goals are, and then invest in their growth. During one-on-one check-ins, listen to their ideas and allow them to lead on ideas that will benefit the business.

Applying McClelland's Theory on Motivation

In applying the work of David McClelland (1961) and his theory of motivation, my experience is that it has been an excellent model to reward and motivate my people and keep them stimulated and engaged. At the heart of McClelland's theory are three basic needs that form human behaviour:

- The need for achievement.
- The need for affiliation.
- The need for power.

The Need for Achievement.

The need for achievement is the first need identified in McClelland's theory of motivation. The need for achievement refers to an individual's needs to achieve or accomplish something worthwhile. For instance, I have always encouraged my team to pursue further knowledge and gain qualifications to support them in their role. My experience is that people who have a need for achievement develop into becoming creative thinkers and or leaders. They are able to find solutions to complex problems and always complete work on time. I have also found that people who seek achievement prefer activities and tasks that can be difficult. From experience, people who have a need for achievement also welcome receiving feedback. They like to know that they are doing a good job, but they also appreciate constructive negative feedback. The need for achievement is something that I have always sought to instil into the mindset of my employees. You cannot assume that achievement is a need that everyone possesses, though it is a need that can be encouraged.

The Need for Affiliation.

The need for affiliation, McClelland's second need, is concerned with people wanting to have good personal relationships with others. In my experience, individuals with a high need for affiliation are sociable and enjoy working in teams. A high need for affiliation is a key trait that I seek when recruiting, as I believe building long-lasting relationships is a cornerstone for success. It is necessary to consider how those who seek affiliation can have opposing values and beliefs to those who seek high achievement. It is essential to have those who need to achieve in a successful company, and it can be challenging to find a balance between these two needs! A generalisation can be made that those individuals with a high need for achievement often have a low need for affiliation, though this is not necessarily the case. Even where this exists, it is the role of leadership to overcome any possible conflict through the steadfast implementation of an organisation's beliefs and values. My experience is that those who have a high need for affiliation conform perfectly to a company's beliefs and values.

Though they adapt immediately to an organisation's culture, they can be hesitant in challenging ideas and processes out of the fear of rejection. This requires the investment of management time to encourage a change in mindset from one of hesitancy to decisiveness.

The Need for Power.

The need for power refers to the need to hold positions of power and authority. My experience is that such people seek to influence, contribute to ideas and provide solutions. Though they make great leaders, as they are ambitious and competitive, care must be applied in their development and the autonomy they are afforded. People who seek the need for power can find it extremely difficult to accept their failures or opposition from other people. Though every business needs people who seek power, and this should be encouraged, business management have a significant part to play in ensuring that they are respectful of the power they have been provided. As long as individuals in a position of power and authority are mentored closely, a business can be rewarded with people who are motivated and able to grow into a leadership role without causing upset and disrupting its organisational culture. A motivated team needs to have a balance of all three needs, and they need to work together as depicted in the following model:

From my experience:

- The need to achieve should be a management priority, to instil and encourage confidence in every member of their team.
- The need for affiliation is the single most significant need for a business to succeed. People with a high need for affiliation do not require interpersonal skills training - and this is crucial in delivering a company's mission and living by its vision, beliefs and values.
- If too many people have a high need for power, the team will suffer from conflict.

Management should always aim to work towards meeting the individual needs of all their people to ensure that all members of a team are motivated to achieve success and growth. My experience is that McClelland's theory on motivation offers insightful guidance into the execution of a reward management strategy.

Culture Redefined

Working Towards Six o'clock
Beyond the Bottom Line

Introduction

In recent times, society has become increasingly aware and concerned about social injustice and environmental issues. The wealth divide, whether it be local, national, or globally, and lack of historic action to tackle climate change has manifested itself to a point where change is now demanded, and rightly so, which has been further exacerbated by the COVID-19 pandemic.

Irrespective of the industry and sector, businesses have a significant role in reducing social and wealth disparity and environmental damage. Since 2020, the acceleration and application of the Environmental, Social and Corporate Governance (ESG) metric that measures sustainability credentials has become a key focus area for large organisations. Regardless of size, business owners and leaders have the influence to play a part in change for the better, and to what extent should be clearly identified in a company's vision. Protecting the environment and supporting those vulnerable in society should be considered a core strategic aim of any business. For leaders who can influence improvements, it should be embedded into the DNA of their decisions.

Playing a part in correcting environmental and social matters is often termed as Corporate and Social Responsibility (CSR), where a company may produce a statement that lives in the depths of a website.

Large companies and some smaller companies often update their CSR position annually to identify targets being achieved. Examples include the use of recycled paper, LED lighting, and promoting amongst their employees the use of cars that emit lower emissions. Such examples, though laudable, do not go far enough, and the way in which environmental improvements are communicated to a business's people is often done in a secondary manner. After all, the traditional and primary aim of a business is to provide a return to its shareholders. This form of promoting CSR, where a business actually focuses the majority or all of its efforts on financial metrics, is traditional capitalism. The time for this to change has arrived.

Regardless of the size of a business, it is the sum of the parts that will make a real difference in addressing social and environmental issues. The most impactful way that a business and its leaders can make a difference is through a paradigm shift from a capitalist model to making stakeholder capitalism central to a company's vision. This can be achieved by centralising CSR as a key objective and engaging with its people, local and wider communities, and customers.

Readdressing social and environmental issues is critical.
If committed to establishing and operating a business, management focus should not solely be on the bottom line. We have entered a changing world where everyone has a responsibility to address social and environmental issues. By focussing beyond-the-bottom-line, investing in and living an inspiring vision, a business will be recognised as pioneers in the stakeholder capitalist movement. Through inclusive participation across a business, the resultant effect will be an increase in team motivation and morale.

A word of caution. If a business's management is not totally committed to social and environmental change, there is no point in expending any time or resource into CSR. This will be greenwashing, and eventually, it will become visible that any endeavours are false. This will lead to a loss of respect, and it could lead to a reduction in motivation amongst an organisation's people. Generation Z, in particular, who are the future of any business, are acutely aware of social and environmental issues that the world faces, and they are people who need inspiring leaders. In not fully supporting change to a stakeholder capitalist future that thinks beyond-the-bottom-line, there is a failure to the next generation, both as an employer and a leader they look up to.

Sustainable Development Goals

Sustainable Development Goals (SDGs) are a collection of seventeen global goals set by the United Nations General Assembly. They are a universal call to action to end poverty, protect the planet and improve the lives and prospects of everyone, everywhere. No better solution in a business playing their part in addressing social and environmental issues as part of beyond-the-bottom-line initiatives exists past the United Nations SDGs. The seventeen goals and how a business can incorporate them into its DNA, along with their intangible benefits, are explored in this chapter.

SDG 1 - No Poverty

Think locally and beyond! A simple way would be to donate money, food, or clothes to charity. A business, through the collective strength of its people, can do more, which can raise a company's profile. Identify and form relationships with charities aligned to No Poverty and volunteer time and, if possible, the organisation's services to charity.

SDG 2 - Zero Hunger

Similar to No Poverty, think local and beyond! Align a business with a charity and build a relationship to play a part in achieving zero hunger.

SDG 3 – Good Health and Wellbeing

Think internally! A business will only thrive and grow if its people are in good health, both physically and mentally. A company that thinks beyond-the-bottom-line should place its people's health and wellbeing above all other business activities.

SDG 4 – Quality Education

Think internally and externally! A forward-thinking business will provide learning and development opportunities to all of its employees. An organisation will be repaid with high levels of motivation when it takes a responsible approach to its people having the right skills to execute their role successfully. From an external perspective, think about how an organisation can align with schools and other education providers – donate money, provide teaching sessions about the industry that it operates in – this could inspire young people to want to forge a career in the company's industry sector.

SDG 5 – Gender Equality

Think internally and diversity! Promote the business's beliefs and values externally. Build a team that represents a cross-section of society – bring together different nationalities, cultures and genders. Be seen as pioneers in overcoming inequalities and discrimination in the workplace. There is no better satisfaction than seeing a diverse team working in harmony together: it solidifies and maintains a best-in-class culture.

SDG 6 – Clean Water and Sanitation

Think beyond! In western society, thought towards clean water and sanitation is rarely considered – we are very fortunate, and we should be thankful. It is estimated that over two billion out of a global population of 7.5 billion do not have access to fresh water. This figure is not palatable, and a business can provide support in third-world emerging nations through supporting the many charities who work tirelessly to reduce this figure. Form a relationship with a reputable charity, and for a modest donation, a business can play its part in increasing the number of people who have access to clean water and sanitation. Let the next generation form these relationships - it will support their development, and they can take pride in taking a lead in the worthiest of causes.

SDG 7 - Affordable and Clean Energy

Think internally! Seek out low carbon energy sources - natural gas supplies are reducing, along with society's reliance on fossil fuels. As an example, for a company's heating needs, think about heat pump technology. Learn how it works and its environmental benefits, and promote low carbon technologies as an affordable and clean source of energy.

SDG 8 - Decent Work and Economic Growth

Think internally! All organisations want a motivated and totally committed team. Provide the best opportunities for your people and constantly seek out ways to develop their skills. This, in turn, will create opportunities in the services that the company provides. It is not just admirable to pay people well, it is the right thing to do, and this is essential to ensure lasting success.

SDG 9 - Industry Innovation and Infrastructure

Think externally and internally! Consider what the business is doing to support industry. Is it innovative? If not, why not? Aim to become innovators. Learn, discuss, educate and promote sustainable infrastructure internally within the workplace. This costs nothing but will focus minds on environmental stewardship, a bedrock of high-quality CSR.

SDG 10 - Reduced Inequalities

Similar to Gender Equality, think internally and diversity! Encourage accountability and responsibility throughout a team, irrespective of race, gender, disability, age, or sexuality. All people are created as equals - there should be no stereotypical dominant type of person in a business.

SDG 11 - Sustainable Cities and Communities

Think internally! It is the sum of the parts that will contribute and ensure a sustainable future. Think about generated waste; can it be recycled or reused? If it can, then do so! Do not leave it to one or a small number of people; management should play their part in recycling and reusing: set a precedent and inspire. A business's people will take their workplace behaviours home and replicate sustainable thinking practices in all aspects of their lives.

SDG 12 - Responsible Consumption and Production

Think internally! Again, it is the sum of the parts that will contribute and ensure a sustainable future. As an example, does something need to be printed? If it is not essential, then do not print it! If people travel as part of their role, think about how sustainability can be encouraged. An easy and effective way is to provide reusable travel cups as opposed to disposable plastic cups. A further advantage is that many hospitality businesses will offer a discount for individuals using their own cup.

SDG 13 - Climate Action

Think internally and externally! A current aspiration of many companies is to be carbon neutral, and an easy way to achieving this goal is through offsetting its business emissions through working with and donating money to charities or organisations that will plant trees on your behalf. A flip side benefit to this is that an organisation can task one of their next-generation team to work out and calculate its emissions. They will take pride in knowing they have played a valuable part and led the cause of being carbon neutral on an annual basis.

SDG 14 - Life Below Water

Think internally and externally! A great way to play a part in improving life below water is by participating in beach clean-ups. Events are organised regularly, and companies are encouraged to help out. Not only will a company be helping our natural environment, but activities like beach cleaning also serve to act as an excellent team-bonding activity, so it will also enhance its organisational culture.

SDG 15 - Life on Land

Think internally! Committing to this goal can be really easy and can make a significant difference. As an example, the web browser Ecosia plant 3,000 a day – make Ecosia the web browser of choice. Encourage a company's people to use public transport, and to drive cars that have low emissions. If possible, invest in cycle to work initiatives to further reduce emissions.

SDG 16 - Peace, Justice and Strong Institutions

Think internally and externally! Simply deliver the organisation's mission, and live by its vision, beliefs and values at all times – instil what the business stands for to its employees, customers, and external peers the business works with. In doing so, the company and its people will be respected as a company with a true social conscience.

SDG 17 - Partnerships for the Goals

Think externally! Seek out other stakeholders who have a similar vision, beliefs and values. Form partnerships with people and organisations that actively encourage social and environmental stewardship. A tangible benefit in doing so can be that new business opportunities are created.

Apply SDGs as a beyond-the-bottom-line initiative.
The application of SDGs is limitless. Their use at an individual company level is open to interpretation, and they cover all aspects of high-quality CSR. As they are led by the United Nations, anyone can relate to them, and most people will have heard about them. In adopting SDGs, an organisation will set out on what can be a continuous journey aligned to the aims of stakeholder capitalism. On attaining a particular goal, replace it with a new one, and encourage participation from all of a business's people. A company CSR policy should involve everyone, and so long as goals are fun and impactful, its culture will benefit through increased levels of motivation and teamwork. Always ensure that social and environmental successes are visible. Publish SDG successes on a company website and its social media channels to promote the good work that the business has carried out.

Continuity and Not Just a Fad

In linking a company vision to activities that think beyond-the-bottom-line, management will need to create a sense of purpose that is shared by their team. This will support the ongoing continuity and relevance of its CSR activities. There are countless examples where CSR fades into the background of a business's objectives and effectively becomes a fad. Whilst any company's primary objective is to be profitable and retain people in meaningful jobs, business leaders and their people should feel a moral obligation to play their part in social and environmental issues.

In connecting CSR to a company's vision and recruiting people who buy into the company mission, vision, beliefs and values, management will be able to rely on them committing additional hours at times to ensure its CSR goals are achieved. Successful CSR and beyond-the-bottom-line initiatives are a fantastic way to publicise and market the work and efforts of a company and its people. Though intangible, it will keep the business at the forefront of the industry that it operates in.

Effective CSR provides publicity and marketing opportunities. CSR requires commitment and time to create a unique platform and initiative that links to the company vision and includes all of its people. High-quality CSR will provide an organisation with positive publicity and marketing opportunities, and it will also increase motivation and team spirit. However, if a business's leaders are not totally committed to CSR, there is little point in embarking on a continuous journey; this is simply greenwashing.

Teamwork and Morale

Aside from making a difference to social inequalities and the environment, the biggest impact from having a CSR initiative that is embedded in a business's DNA is the positivity, increase in motivation and team spirit amongst its people. People want to work for a company that cares and thinks beyond making a profit for its shareholders. A continuous initiative will also provide the next generation, who invariably have lower cost overheads and more time than experienced people, an opportunity to take the lead on critically important work. Not only does this enhance levels of motivation, but it also prepares them for an increase in responsibility as they gain knowledge and experience. Additionally, it will help management to identify those who will become future leaders of the business.

Applying STEEPLE to support Beyond the Bottom Line Initiatives

A measure of ensuring the continuity of your vision, beliefs and values, where you think beyond-the-bottom-line, is to identify what and how you can be involved in playing a part in addressing external social inequalities and improving the environment.

The STEEPLE framework is a technique to identify changes that take place within that environment. The categories within the framework are Social, Technological, Economic, Environmental, Political, Legal and Ethical. The analysis focuses on aspects of the environment that may affect or influence an organisation. Although similar to a PEST (Political, Economic, Social and Technological) analysis, I believe that the application of STEEPLE is more pertinent due to the inclusion of Environmental, Legal and Ethical considerations, owing to the current day significance of sustainability, equity and fairness. In my opinion, the STEEPLE framework can also further support the necessary changes required globally that have been exacerbated by the COVID-19 pandemic. The framework is contextualised below and on the following page, explaining how it can relate and be connected to a company's CSR initiatives and work in synergy and towards a progressive stakeholder capitalist future.

Social

The Great Reset is a proposal by the World Economic Forum (WEF) to rebuild the economy sustainably following the COVID-19 pandemic. It was unveiled in May 2020 by Prince Charles and the WEF director, Klaus Schwab. It seeks to improve capitalism by making investments more geared towards mutual progress and focusing more on environmental initiatives. Focusing on the Great Reset and SDGs demonstrates high-quality CSR that can be embedded into a company's DNA, ensuring that it is a continuous beyond-the-bottom-line programme.

Technological

Technology is a wide area, and in simplistic terms, that assumes a business is a user of technology as opposed to an innovator of technology. The COVID-19 pandemic has demonstrated that business can continue in the form of video calls (VC) instead of face-to-face meetings. Continuing to use VC technology post-pandemic will help support the aim of reducing emissions connected with travel.

Economic

Economic factors linked to CSR initiatives, such as working with SDGs, could relate to education and training in both internal and external environments. Developing employees through them gaining experience and knowledge will lead to an increased skillset and possible diversity in services provided; therefore, indirectly supporting business growth. Externally, supporting schools or charities with funding to purchase educational books, or providing workshops about what a business does, could inspire a future generation to enter a well-paid industry with wide economic benefits.

Environmental

Understanding the impact that a business has on the natural environment is the first step towards improvement. A continuous CSR programme will allow the benchmarking of the current status linked to energy use and emissions (from energy consumption and travel) and support decisions to reduce a business's energy consumption and emissions year on year.

Political

Local and global political spectrums will focus on a post-COVID-19 world. Being aligned to progressive ideals such as stakeholder capitalism and the Great Reset and linking them to marketing activities will showcase a company's beyond-the-bottom-line efforts, earning plaudits and possibly attracting new business.

Legal

Though there are no legal connotations connected to CSR initiatives, it does not mean that there will not be a request for any business to record and report its environmental impact in the future. Preparing through doing the right thing by the environment will demonstrate stewardship and a pioneering spirit of a business.

Ethical

Being seen as a socially and environmentally conscious organisation may create further business opportunities as society as a whole becomes increasingly aware and concerned about the environment and social inequalities.

Summary

In my experience, creating a vision that focuses on the environment and instilling beliefs and values that consider social inequalities has significant benefits. By linking Corporate Social Responsibility initiatives with the Sustainable Development Goals, team spirit is enhanced by promoting inclusive participation, high morale and an increase in motivation. Externally, the business is considered as an industry pioneer that focuses beyond-the-bottom-line and has synergy with the aims of 'Build Back Better', a campaign fighting for change due to the COVID-19 pandemic.

It is a proud feeling to play a part in correcting social and environmental concerns that are increasingly coming to the fore of society as a consequence of the COVID-19 pandemic.

Working Towards Seven o'clock
Measurement

Introduction

A point in time will be reached where a business has a core nucleus of experienced professionals who have played their part in its success, and its next generation talent can significantly contribute with less mentoring and guidance. To ensure a business is positioned for successful growth, it is critical to assess the current position on organisational culture and leadership as the experience across a team increases. Assessment will identify the good, the bad and the ugly, and management need to be prepared for this! It is likely that an organisation's management will have a feel for what they, the business, and its people do well. Assessment will identify these areas plus those that require improvement and provide a plan to where a business should be taken.

The Investors in People© We invest in people accreditation is a globally recognised mark of excellence, particularly in the areas of leading, supporting and improving people. Accreditation serves two purposes: if accredited, it provides an opportunity for positive publicity and marketing opportunities, and secondly, but more crucially, it will highlight the areas of improvement that a business should be focussing on. Where a business is seeking to develop and grow, understanding and having its culture assessed is essential. Management must be prepared for the assessment's outputs, as an organisation's culture is directly linked to its leadership, and necessary improvements are their responsibility.

Investors in People© performance and measurement areas cover three distinct indicators: Leading, Supporting and Improving, and these indicators have nine sub-indicators, identified below:

Leadership

- Leading and inspiring people
- Living the organisation's behaviours and values
- Empowering and involving people

Supporting

- Managing performance
- Recognising and rewarding performance
- Structuring performance

Improving

- Building capability
- Delivering continuous improvement
- Creating sustainable success

In setting up, or having set-up, or being employed to run a business, it is incredible how pertinent the nine indicators are, and how relevant they are for any company that aims to place organisational culture as its key strategy.

All indicators are assessed as part of the process to measure a business's culture. The assessment takes a two-fold approach. Anonymous surveys are sent to the organisation's people, where each survey question is answered on a scale of strongly agree to strongly disagree. Following the collation of the survey results, depending on the organisation's size, all, or a random selection of its people, are interviewed by an expert Investors in People© practitioner. The practitioner will then collate all of their findings into a report, highlighting the alignments to the We invest in people framework and particularly which stage the organisation is in for each indicator: Developed, Established, Advanced or High Performing.

Accepting feedback and improving.
It is important to remember when receiving assessment feedback that the business invited Investors in People© into its inner workings, and all the representatives are experienced in the field of business management. Listen and act on feedback, no matter how trivial or, in some areas, how unpalatable it may be! Investors in People© want companies to succeed and thrive and are positioned and exist to support organisations seeking to improve. Ultimately, improvements in organisational culture will reflect positively on the goods and services that a business provides to its customers.

Establish the Current Position on Leadership and Culture

Establishing how effective an organisation's leadership and culture are and where improvements are required can be used as a catalyst for growth and decide the path that a company takes into its future. Firstly, consider its leaders. Do they inspire people? Assuming an organisation has received an assessment that confirms leaders do, seek ways in which further inspiration can be delivered to its people. Business owners and senior leaders work tirelessly to establish and maintain a respected business. Leadership may already be good, but to take a defined path that allows further growth will either require a realignment or being more vocal about the mission, vision, beliefs and values of an organisation. Continuous communication of what the company stands for is essential in guiding employees and being seen as an inspirational and motivational leader.

In a company that seeks to implement an industry-leading culture, its leaders must understand how to manage the performance of all its people and improve its current position of culture. In theory, improving performance is easy – inspire people, set goals, and communicate with them regularly. Day-to-day activities, or getting the job done, and problems that require addressing will always occur, but these are no reason not to communicate with an organisation's people. Away from annual or twice-yearly appraisals that will be used to set performance expectations and goals, be regimented, and set time aside for regular one-to-one meetings with an organisation's people. This is a great way to listen and provide inspiration and mentoring to keep people motivated.

Regular one-to-one meetings interlaced with appraisal reviews are the most effective way to build the capability of a business and its people and deliver continuous improvement. Human nature is such that everyone responds positively to being involved and acknowledged for a job well done. As long as individual improvements in performance are communicated constructively, a level of appreciation will always be acknowledged through an individual or team performance output. Importantly, always provide praise and recognition and share individual efforts with all of the team. Put people on a pedestal when they have delivered an excellent job or gone above and beyond the call of duty.

Creating sustainable success.
Measuring the position on leadership and culture and continuously seeking ways to improve from a top-down perspective is key to growing, thriving and creating sustainable success. A business's people are central to how good its culture is, which is directly linked to the leadership and management provided. Think 'inspirational' by always following and instilling the mission and live by the organisation's vision, beliefs and values. Involve and empower an organisation's people, provide regular feedback, build their capabilities, and above all, be a leader who listens and learns to ensure that success is sustained and not simply short term.

Making Good Better

Receiving independent verification and an assessment of an organisation's leadership and culture and establishing its position will assist decisions surrounding improvements and set a clear path and journey of growth. In the example of Investors in People© accreditation, this can play a key part in attracting talent to a business. People need to feel valued and want to work in a top-class environment. Accreditation, assuming that a company markets and publicises it, demonstrates that, when it comes to leadership and organisational culture, the business is ahead of its competition. Effectively, a company can now say with credibility that it has strong leadership and a people-centric culture. Management should rightly celebrate the company-wide efforts with all of its people; consider it a promotion to the premier league, where the business is now aiming to be better and aspiring to be the best.

As a company embarks on this new phase of its journey, recap, revisit and, if necessary, improve its strategy by design. Is the mission clear and still relevant? Is it customer orientated? Does it demonstrate that the business is an industry leader? Does it send a clear modus operandi, e.g., that the organisation represents quality and value? Is the company vision clear and relevant? Is it aspirational, and does it compliment beyond-the-bottom-line endeavours? Having a genuine social and environmental conscience is going to be crucial in a post-COVID-19 world. Ask if the business is still living by its beliefs and values. These should not change, but they should be focal to the business. In aiming to be better and raising the bar when it comes to leadership and culture, thought should be given to how management communicate and should consider:

- Introducing visual art in the workplace that reinforces the business's culture, mission, vision, beliefs and values.
- Introducing regular newsletters and celebrating individual and team successes. Discuss current work activities and growth strategies – inform and include all of an organisation's people.

- Ensuring that the company has effective two-way communication mechanisms between management and all of its people.
- It is management's responsibility to ensure that its people feel inspired and motivated to deliver the organisation's goals. Consider ways to develop further the effectiveness of communication throughout a company. Encourage people to have the confidence to openly discuss and contribute to the business.
- In terms of line management, people need to be aware of who their line manager is, what support they will receive from them and how they work together. Many people in a young company will display an emotional need to have input and line management from its founder. As a company grows, the role of the founder will have to change, and re-enforcing the line management structure will help 'unfasten' people from these emotional attachments to the founder.
- It is likely that company leaders have values that subconsciously underpin how they behave and make decisions. As management seek to be better and to grow, it is worthwhile considering the introduction of more conscious management techniques to ensure people act and behave in line with the company's beliefs and values – such as those introduced in this chapter.
- Welcome feedback as a gift into an organisation's culture. It is possible that its people could be awestruck by their leaders and the business's achievements. There could be a subconscious belief that management would never require feedback on how to improve. This is never the case. Leadership that is provided to an organisation's people can always be better.
- There could also be a tendency for a defensive emotional reaction to challenging feedback, both receiving it and being asked to provide it. Being accountable for giving feedback and having challenging conversations is something that should be prioritised in terms of developing its people.

As a company grows, management need to aim to be better and ensure that it provides its people with well-designed, interesting and structured job roles to deliver the company objectives. Provide people with training and development opportunities to support them in developing skills and knowledge. Provide them with opportunities that will allow them to move into other roles and ensure that knowledge transfer is promoted from experienced employees to those people new to a role. Maintain a passion for delivering continuous improvement through ensuring that the business's people are enthusiastic and are committed to supporting the improvement in the quality of goods and services provided to its customers.

Becoming better.
It is the organisational culture that will lead a business to become better. Measuring its position and understanding where and how to improve will guide the company as it grows, so long as its mission, vision, beliefs and values are followed. As it expands, its structures and people will have to adapt to change. Effective, open and clear communication will be key to its continued success. Two-way feedback is essential to ensure that the core foundations and underlying principles of the business remain in the quest of becoming better.

Applying Deming's PDCA Cycle to Measure Leadership and Culture

From my experience, a measure of success in becoming better is through a structured and continuous appraisal of organisational culture and leadership once its current position is established. Following accreditation as an Investors in People© company, the structured and continuous system I applied was through the work of W. Edwards Deming from the 1950s.

Deming's continuous PDCA quality improvement model of Plan, Do, Check and Act, provided me with a logical sequence to ensure further improvements were made. I applied each stage in terms of improving my organisational culture and leadership, and this is depicted in the following model:

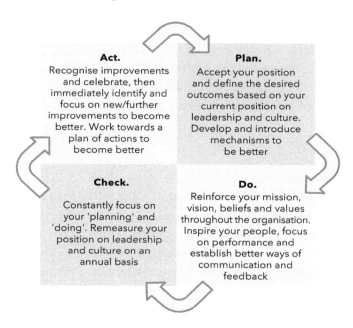

Act.
Recognise improvements and celebrate, then immediately identify and focus on new/further improvements to become better. Work towards a plan of actions to become better

Plan.
Accept your position and define the desired outcomes based on your current position on leadership and culture. Develop and introduce mechanisms to be better

Check.
Constantly focus on your 'planning' and 'doing'. Remeasure your position on leadership and culture on an annual basis

Do.
Reinforce your mission, vision, beliefs and values throughout the organisation. Inspire your people, focus on performance and establish better ways of communication and feedback

Through increased leadership engagement and two-way feedback communication introduced as a result of applying the theory of PDCA, I found that the organisational culture and leadership of WAVE became better. Our Investors in People© assessment resulted in a score of 834 out of 900. The benchmark score for accreditation is 724. Following a conscious effort to become better through studying and linking the work of Deming resulted in an assessment score of 866 just twelve months later. This is expanded in detail in Chapter 12.

An Investors in People© assessment fulfils the old adage that you have to be able to measure it if you want to be able to manage it! Their assessment allowed me to manage and plan for the future.

Working Towards Eight o'clock
Planning for The Future

Introduction

Chapter 8 represents a change in direction for Culture Redefined. Going forward, the narrative is concerned with the future. It focuses on establishing and introducing a paradigm shift in how a business can increase its success and position itself for longevity by moving away from a traditional operating model to one that focuses on stakeholder capitalism. From experience, this paradigm relies upon and assumes that a business has or is willing to centralise its business strategy around its culture. Chapter 8 begins with a recap of lessons learnt in being able to plan for the future:

Reaching One o'clock – Strategy by Design

- An aspirational mission statement is in place and is central to the business.
- The company vision sets long-term goals and focuses on having a social and environmental conscience.
- Beliefs and values are core to a business's culture that aims to serve customers to the best of its ability by creating a winning team, and where the company's inner workings constantly strive to be better. All of an organisation's people centralise integrity, respect, teamwork, communication, a quest for excellence, being accountable and trust at the heart of everything that they do.

- Young members of a team, the next generation, are given the opportunity to accept responsibility, lead and shine.

Reaching Two o'clock – Marketing by Design

- Ensure that the company's shop window, its website, is current, informative and kept up to date. Social media platforms should be used to showcase success to a wide audience.
- The products or services provided by an organisation solve a customer's problems.
- The pricing of products and services is clear and consistent. They provide a profit, but more importantly, they represent quality and value.
- Products or services are provided in appropriate geographical regions.
- Marketing focuses on initiatives that are beyond the traditional bottom line. Stakeholder capitalism is introduced to demonstrate that the company is passionate about its role in improving societal and environmental matters.
- Leaders are visible in ensuring customer satisfaction, and they seek to build lasting relationships.
- Management monitors the organisation's macro environment, are aware of what its competition is doing and of new market entrants. The company consistently demonstrates that it is better than its competitors.

Reaching Three o'clock – Growth

- Transformational leadership is the bedrock of the management of the business. Leaders promote intellectual stimulation to encourage creativity.
- Support is provided to an organisation's people to ensure that their ideas are listened to.
- Leaders motivate their people, adhere strictly to the business's mission, vision, beliefs and values, and aspire to instil the same passion into employees in meeting individual and organisational goals.

Reaching Four o'clock – The Next Generation

- Once an experienced team has been established and is working in harmony with the business's mission, vision, beliefs and values, recruitment takes a different path: the company builds and moulds its own people, the next generation.
- Increasing a business's capacity through developing the next generation is highly rewarding. Management needs to be patient, display enthusiasm and energy, and make time to mentor young people.
- Set goals and formally review performance twice a year. In addition, provide constant communication and be visible, approachable and give feedback on a regular basis.
- Assess early day leadership qualities by allowing the next generation to lead initiatives connected to the company's vision.
- Ensure everyone in the organisation supports the development of the next generation.
- A Power-based culture is introduced and is blended with a Task-based culture. Task culture is crucial in planning for and implementing future change in the operating model of any business that aspires to the aims of stakeholder capitalism.

Reaching Five o'clock – Reward Management

- Outdated paradigms that focus solely on competitive pay are not sufficient to guarantee productivity, profitability, or survival.
- Motivation is key. Trust people. Give people purpose. Be positive. Be transparent. Have an open-door policy. Let people lead. Show people the bigger picture. Recognise and praise a job well done.
- Transformational leadership and motivation are the key ingredients to successful reward management. It is important to recognise that individual rewards will be circumstance based – all an organisation's people will have different wants and needs.

Reaching Six o'clock – Beyond-the-Bottom-Line

- Create a vision connected to correcting social and environmental issues, but do not greenwash. Action is required now, and business leaders have the ability to play a significant role in correcting past mistakes.
- Embed what the company does to improve sociological and environmental issues into its DNA.
- Centralise CSR as a core organisational objective and involve the business's people, customers and the local and wider communities.
- A company that truly thinks and embarks on a beyond-the-bottom-line journey will enjoy an increase in team motivation and morale. The business will be seen as pioneers by its customers and by the local and wider communities. This could present bottom-line-impacting opportunities from playing the organisation's part in doing the right thing.

Reaching Seven o'clock – Measurement

- Evaluate through external measurement the business's position as it relates to leadership and organisational culture.
- Seek ways to improve how to lead, inspire and live by the company's beliefs and values.
- Seek ways to improve how management supports its people. Manage performance better by recognising and rewarding performance. Take communication to elevated levels in the continuous quest to become better.
- Management should seek ways to enhance how to build further capability throughout the team, remain steadfast in delivering continuous improvement, and set in motion a plan of how they are going to execute sustainable success.
- Apply external assessment and its findings linked to the current position on leadership and culture to set a plan in motion for the future.

In planning for the future, this chapter now focuses on skill set regarding delegating responsibilities, the importance of promotion, and why continuous change is crucial in the continuing success of a business.

Responsibilities by Skill Set

A skill set combines knowledge, personal qualities and abilities that are developed over time and acquired in personal and work life. A skill set combines two types of skills: soft skills and hard skills.

Soft skills are interpersonal, people-driven skills. They are not particularly quantifiable and, when it comes to successful recruitment, the skills that management should look for are good communication, listening, attention to detail, the ability to learn, think critically, empathetically, and conflict resolution abilities. Hard skills are teachable. They are quantifiable by their nature through knowledge transfer and skills acquired over a period of time. In the workplace, everyone will use a range of skills every day. Some of these skills are job-specific and will be taught through a blend of on-the-job training, mentoring and gaining qualifications.

The importance of soft skills when recruiting the next generation.
Time waits for no one. Even at the point of recruiting the next generation, management will be well placed in considering an individual's soft skills over those that are quantifiable, such as qualifications. The success of any business relies on its ability to resolve problems, and being customer-facing is critical. There is a direct correlation between the speed at which the business can place its people in front of your customers and the success and growth of your business.

Recognising the skill sets amongst an organisation's people is crucial, especially when responsibility is delegated. Do not underestimate the power of soft skills, particularly when recruiting the next generation, as successful interaction and communication are key to any business's success. To guarantee longevity and when planning for the future, the business is going to have to rely on its young people extensively. Role-specific, or hard skills, can be taught and developed over time. However, where there is a specific need for high-quality interpersonal skills, as required for customer-facing roles, a company's recruitment process will play a significant part. Management should place emphasis on gauging how quickly its young people will develop, specifically relating to them taking on senior responsibilities within the business.

A Clear Path to Promotion

Promoting people plays a significant role in the continued success of any business. Specifically relating to a business's young people, the next generation, where customers have indirectly played a role in their development, there is no greater satisfaction for the company and customers alike than seeing the next generation flourish. It is rewarding to see them take on responsibility, play their role in solving customer problems and contribute to decision-making.

In planning for the future by rewarding young people through promotion and giving them responsibility, management instil a sense of pride in their people, and demonstrate the business's trust in them. The resultant effect, even though life experience may be lacking, is that the company will be rewarded with loyal and motivated employees. They will have an unparalleled thirst to solve the most difficult of problems that come with responsibility. Young people who have climbed and continue to climb the career ladder will still require mentoring. However, the rate at which they develop into a senior role through the faith placed in them will reduce the amount of time they require mentoring as they will want to repay the business.

Plan for the future and focus on promotion.
Business never stands still: change is a continuous process. At all times, keep an eye on the future and encourage people to grow into roles with added layers of responsibility. Promotion sends a clear message to the industry that hard work is rewarded and that the business has a continued succession plan and the ability to grow successfully.

Promotion also sends a clear message throughout a business: that hard work pays off. In planning for the future, if the company has a continued programme of recruiting young people, they will see from the very first day that opportunities exist in the business. This will serve to encourage their growth and development.

Applying the Moorhead and Griffin Change Agent Model to Initiate Change

In planning for the future, no matter if, as a business leader, you have no immediate exit plan, you should at all times consider succession planning to ensure business longevity. In creating a business that has centralised culture at its core, your plan has to be focused on its continued success and longevity. Whether you like it or not, you should place focus on the business having the ability to continue and succeed without you.

In my role as a business leader, I have considered myself as a change agent in respect of planning for the future. An approach I have taken from my academic learnings is applying the work of Moorhead and Griffin. McKenna (2000) advocates Moorhead and Griffin's Change Agent model as it examines organisational change from the perspective of top management. Change in this instance relates to how I have prepared my business for a long and successful future through considering myself as a change agent in delivering my company mission and living by its vision, beliefs and values.

Successful and continuous change relies on a best-in-class culture where these goals are central to its operation.

My experience of establishing and building a successful business that focuses on continuous change in planning for the future is that instilling a company's mission, vision, beliefs and values into its DNA encourages the acceptance of responsibility amongst its people. In considering leadership being a subconscious change agent within a people-centric organisation, it will ensure that no one person is irreplaceable and that a company can continue to succeed long into the future.

The following model depicts the role of the change agent in respect of planning for the future:

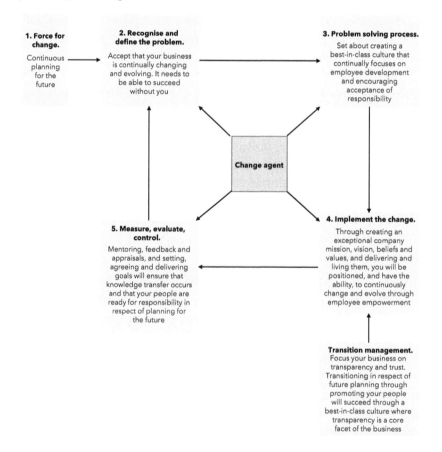

1. Force for change.
Continuous planning for the future

2. Recognise and define the problem.
Accept that your business is continually changing and evolving. It needs to be able to succeed without you

3. Problem solving process.
Set about creating a best-in-class culture that continually focuses on employee development and encouraging acceptance of responsibility

Change agent

5. Measure, evaluate, control.
Mentoring, feedback and appraisals, and setting, agreeing and delivering goals will ensure that knowledge transfer occurs and that your people are ready for responsibility in respect of planning for the future

4. Implement the change.
Through creating an exceptional company mission, vision, beliefs and values, and delivering and living them, you will be positioned, and have the ability, to continuously change and evolve through employee empowerment

Transition management.
Focus your business on transparency and trust. Transitioning in respect of future planning through promoting your people will succeed through a best-in-class culture where transparency is a core facet of the business

Working Towards Nine o'clock
COVID-19

Introduction

In early 2020, the world changed. The COVID-19 pandemic has affected everyone. The anxiety, worry and unpredictability caused by the pandemic are like nothing the majority of people have experienced in living memory. For business owners and leaders, it created a lonely and dark place due to high levels of uncertainty. Many viable and long-standing businesses have failed due to the pandemic, and those businesses that have successfully navigated it will be well-positioned to consider a change in how they operate.

From experience, the single biggest seed of optimism from a business leader's perspective is the knowledge of how much a company means to its people. This should be a catalyst for change, a change where people are rewarded for their loyalty. A great way to start the journey of change is by embracing the Great Reset through introducing and experimenting with the principles of stakeholder capitalism into a business. The World Economic Forum defines stakeholder capitalism as "A form of capitalism in which companies seek long-term value creation by taking into account the needs of all their stakeholders, and society at large". Where an organisation already has a vision, beliefs and values aligned to initiatives that think beyond-the-bottom-line, change and the formal introduction of stakeholder capitalism will be both easy and a natural progression for a business.

Consider COVID-19 as a catalyst for change.
The COVID-19 pandemic brought unthinkable levels of anxiety to the fore of business. Those companies that have navigated the pandemic will now have leaders who understand just how much their business means to its people. Alongside the global shift in adopting the progressive ideals of a stakeholder capitalist future, business leaders will be well-placed to reward their people, focus on correcting social and economic disparity, and prevent environmental catastrophe.

Stakeholder Capitalism

In 2021, there is significant debate as to whether stakeholder capitalism can provide a better way to support and strengthen the economy. With vision, it is easy to see how the progressive ideals of this concept could be embraced by businesses as a forward-thinking and successful operating model. Stakeholder capitalism originates from the work of Hein Kroos and Klaus Schwab, who brought its conception to attention back in 1971. The core of stakeholder capitalism is where a company does not simply prioritise profits for shareholders but seeks long-term value creation by considering the needs of all a business's stakeholders, society and the environment.

The reintroduction of stakeholder capitalism as a business ideal in this instance should be considered as an operating model for further, equitable and fair change for all of its people. Plus, it is an opportunity to play a part in the Great Reset. As a result of the COVID-19 pandemic, everyone in society is facing exacerbated social, economic and environmental concerns. Business owners and leaders can prioritise a new way of working that focuses on rewarding its people whilst supporting social and environmental initiatives, such as adopting the UN's Sustainable Development Goals, as opposed to the self-interest goals of typical capitalism. In implementing the progressive ideals of stakeholder capitalism, a company can be positioned for long-term success and growth.

Stakeholder capitalism can be considered as being directly linked to socialist principles. In the world of business, a blend of capitalism and socialism can work together. This blended concept should not be considered taboo or impossible: it can, and it does work when you think holistically and widely. Traditional capitalism that works in harmony with socialist principles is effectively the foundation of stakeholder capitalism. In 2021, stakeholder capitalism is easier for people to identify with as the world has become a smaller place. Economies, societies and the environment are closely linked to each other. Our planet's future is not dependent on the decisions of a few global leaders but the sum of everyone who is in a position of influence, including small business owners, leaders and their people, who contribute to social, environmental and economic improvements.

At the core of embracing stakeholder capitalism and making changes due to the COVID-19 pandemic, all stakeholders in any walk of life, whether in business or personally, have a collective responsibility to work together to address imbalances of wealth creation and retention for a few. A successful stakeholder future will have to involve and be embraced by everyone from government to businesses, to communities to individuals. They are all interconnected dependents. The wellbeing of people and the environment globally impacts all societies and is the collective responsibility of everyone. In this instance, it should start with a change in how business models operate to address social wellbeing, environmental and economic issues. COVID-19 has exacerbated how fragile society is, but it can also serve as a catalyst and an opportunity for positive change. The pandemic can be considered 'the straw that broke the camel's back'. Over the past twenty-five years, the use of the internet has spread, making us all aware of local and wider disparities, and drawing attention to change being a necessity.

The first eight chapters of this book focused on the importance of centralising culture and leadership in establishing a business, ensuring its success, growth, longevity, how improvements can be made and planning for the future. Though the narrative has started to explore the necessity of change and set the backdrop to current issues, it will now identify how it can be implemented at a business level. The centre of attention now switches and explores a business operating model that can be introduced in redefining organisational culture to ensure success in today's modern world where stakeholder capitalism will play a pivotal role. This operating model is employee ownership and, specifically in this case study, the model is through the formation of an Employee Ownership Trust (EOT).

Embrace and exceed the concept of stakeholder capitalism.
The concept of stakeholder capitalism is not new. However, in today's current climate, where its progressive values are implemented, it can be considered a natural evolution for forward-thinking businesses with a significant societal and environmental conscience. Where there is a leadership ability to recognise the need for change that centralises fairness and equity, organisations will be well placed to implement the core foundations of stakeholder capitalism as a mechanism for long-lasting success and growth. The formation of an EOT could be the solution.

Team Mentality

The earliest and brightest light in the early days of the COVID-19 pandemic, from my experience of operating a small company, was how much the business meant to its people. Similar to many service-based companies, the world of business ground to a screeching halt in late March 2020. Uncertainties were plentiful: anticipate the worst, hope for the best. As soon as the UK government intervened and offered support via the furlough scheme, the decision to take advantage was easy. The scheme offered a means by which to help protect the long-term survival of businesses across the UK.

From an employee's perspective, being placed on furlough and being under a lockdown was a distressing time. This increased the likelihood of mental health issues that will likely be the biggest and most long-term impact once the pandemic has passed. Though furloughed employees were unable to work, from a personal perspective as a leader who places their people as the company's biggest asset, a decision was taken to set aside two hours per week where the whole team – those furloughed and those who continued to work – could meet over a video conference. The majority of time in each of those weekly meetings was spent informally as check-ins, where support was provided to everyone, from everyone, for over three months.

It became apparent how much the business meant to everyone and how motivated they were and remained committed to delivering 100% customer satisfaction. Their passion during this period remained steadfast, and their resolve and positivity grew exponentially. It was at this time when the realisation dawned that something had to change. Rewarding the business's people was going to be absolutely necessary once the first lockdown was over. During this time, employee ownership, specifically the establishment of an EOT, was explored due to its synergy with stakeholder capitalism.

Do not overlook how much your business means to your people.
If the COVID-19 pandemic only taught business owners and leaders one thing, it was hopefully how much a company, its people, and the customers mean to them. This will be clear for any business that places a people-centric culture alongside transformational leadership as key strategic drivers. The most meaningful reward for an organisation's people, and one that will present long-term prosperity benefit for all, whilst truly embracing stakeholder capitalism and the Great Reset, is through employee ownership.

Preparing a Business for The Future

The first stage in transitioning to an employee ownership model is careful consideration from a business's owners. Selling all or a majority shareholding to any party is a significant decision, even more so when exploring employee ownership. Shareholders will have built a fantastic business and brand, and they need to be assured that success will continue when under new ownership.

In some respects, a traditional sale is easier from the perspective of reassurance, as any buyer will either have experience or position one of their own people into a leadership role within a business that they acquire. In employee-owned models, a company's founders and shareholders are reliant on the existing team to step up into leadership roles. However, where a strategy has been designed around its people and culture, and where a business has promoted accountability and responsibility, the likelihood of success in transitioning to employee ownership will be high. From the top-down, it is essential that the business is well placed for change. Where a company has demonstrable proof that it has consistently delivered its mission and lived by its vision, beliefs and values through its people, a change to employee ownership will be embraced and be successful.

Appropriate levels of skill set throughout the team are necessary, as is a positive attitude. When the business becomes employee-owned, its people will have significant influence, and current management must be certain that the business is ready for this change. If there are gaps regarding skill sets during the planning stage, from trainee level to its leaders, these need to be addressed before announcing the intended change to an organisation's employees.

The structure of the business should be assessed, with questions such as, is it fit for the purpose of employee ownership? The obvious assumption would be yes. However, this is a superficial perspective. A plan for a change in structure is necessary. There should be a focus on employees with leadership qualities, and the process of sharing and passing responsibility should begin.

Ensure that change is right for the business.
When considering any change to a business's operating model, it is important to ensure it is the right thing to do from an existing shareholder perspective. The next stage is careful planning and, if exploring employee ownership, it is absolutely critical to plug any skills gaps.

Applying Kubler-Ross Five Stages of Grief in the Context of COVID-19

In preparing for change and transitioning to employee ownership, I applied the work of Kubler-Ross and their Five Stages of Grief model (1973). The catalyst behind the change was the COVID-19 pandemic and inception of the Great Reset, where the progressive ideals of stakeholder capitalism will become more prominent in both business and everyday life.

Fundamental to the successful transition of change in company ownership is its acceptance by both its shareholders and stakeholders. Within this context, the work of Kubler-Ross is pertinent, who argued that all humans go through five stages of grief: denial, anger, bargaining, depression and acceptance when faced with a loss or change. In this instance, the COVID-19 pandemic can be considered as grief. As such, it is deemed relevant to turn a negative into a positive by creating an equitable and fair change that is central to employee ownership business models.

In applying the work of Kubler-Ross, I found it an ideal mechanism to address the personal struggles as a business owner during the first COVID-19 lockdown and to guide communication and support my team through the period of change. How I applied Kubler-Ross' theory in the five-stage process in planning for this change is narrated below:

Denial

In creating a successful business with fantastic people, the first lockdown of 2020 created somewhat of a haze and an inability to grasp the gravity of a situation that I had no control over, leading to a short-term sense of denial.

Anger

The reality of realising that I was in a situation that I had no control over soon turned my thoughts towards anger and frustration. However, borne of my frustration and subsequent realisation of how much the company meant to my employees, a vision of change became apparent. As long as the pandemic could be navigated from a business perspective, which did occur, I set about planning what the future of my business should be.

Bargaining

The bargaining stage was two-fold. Firstly, we had to understand the worth of the business from a financial perspective, and what my wife and I, as shareholders, would expect to achieve through discounting its true value to ensure no debt was incurred on the company in becoming employee-owned. Secondly, on negotiating what a fair and equitable value was, the proposal was presented to my employees as a means of bargaining to gain their buy-in to the change.

Depression

The depression stage is the one stage in respect of change that did not occur to any significant extent. Naturally, subconscious questions play a part in times of consideration regarding change as a way forward and a natural progression. The overriding reflection of subconscious questions was that changing to an employee-owned business model was the correct one, having designed my strategy around organisational culture and how much the company meant to my employees.

Acceptance

The acceptance stage followed the bargaining and negotiation with my people. A series of workshops helped guide the team through what business ownership entailed prior to formalising the legalities. These workshops reinforced that the change was the correct decision and was accepted by everyone. They assured the future would ensure fairness and that equity was at the heart of an already best-in-class culture business.

Summary

The COVID-19 pandemic caused significant levels of anxiety and uncertainty, but it also provided a real opportunity to reflect on my role. It presented an opportunity to plan for the future and create change for the benefit of my employees. The pandemic was the catalyst to prepare for employee ownership. It has significant synergy with the Great Reset and the progressive ideals of stakeholder capitalism. As the movement towards a stakeholder capitalist future gains momentum, employee ownership will provide progressive companies with several opportunities. There will be an ability to attract the best talent and make a business and its services more appealing for existing and new customers, who will also align themselves to a fairer and more equitable future.

Culture Redefined

Working Towards Ten o'clock
Change

Introduction

We are at a turning point in human history. A time when new ideas will arise and old ideas will be revisited. The COVID-19 pandemic has changed the world forever, acting as both an agent of change and an accelerator or catalyst of slowly emerging ideas. Despite the deaths and economic casualties, there has emerged a mighty winner – science. This bodes well for the fight against the threat of climate change.

But it is social inequality that has exploded and will be the prime mover of global change in the coming period. The pandemic has exposed all of the underlying weaknesses in countries, not least in the UK. This is the world that tomorrow's workers will inherit. Alternatives to the given will attract many young people who will come across ideas like employee ownership and see the attraction. If the employee ownership model, and those of a similar nature, are to develop, they have no alternative but to engage in the day-to-day politics of society. All organisations require a legal framework in which to operate. This clearly includes tax regimes, director responsibility and grants for training and staff development. It involves bank rates and interest rates for borrowing and investment. It has to operate within the legal framework of employment rights, equalities legislation and health and safety laws and practices.

Embracing tomorrow's world.
A time for emerging ideas for creating a fairer society and finally tackling climate change is upon us. To ensure the longevity of any business, change is necessary. As a progressive model aligned to the stakeholder capitalist movement, employee ownership will grow, and companies who make this change will have to be vocal. They have a part to play and should impart their ideals in the day-to-day politics of society, as society embraces tomorrow's post-COVID-19 world.

Pioneering Change

All employee-owned organisations need quality professionals from diverse backgrounds to advance the business. Alongside quality and diversity, an organisation's people will need to be committed to a redefined culture, the company's aims and its aspirations. Irrespective of the operating model, to meet the challenges of today that include the breakneck speed of technological change, the UK needs healthy bodies and brains. At the very least, and for this to occur, the country requires a quality health service, a first-class education system open to all regardless of income, and a long-term goal of being free from fear of job loss, redundancy and poverty.

That is why voices are now being raised for a new, post-COVID-19 world. Progressive thinkers are now revisiting the post-war reconstruction of the UK. Like today, World War II ended with massive public debt, which society lived with, albeit with rationing, in the expectation that it would be paid off in the long term. In return for the sacrifices, full employment was promised, plus mass housing built to provide an escape from the slums, with a house for every family.

What is most remembered, though probably not by name, was the Beveridge Report (1942), which sought to eradicate the five great 'giant evils' - Want, Disease, Ignorance, Squalor and Idleness of society. Though the world has changed dramatically since the

1940s, the COVID-19 pandemic has spewed the five giants back onto the surface of UK society. The next generation of workers will emerge from lockdown with a huge diversity of ideas, thoughts and reflections. Some will be scared. Many will have under-achieved. Many will be angry, but others will be raring to go, and employee-owned companies whose mission, vision, beliefs and values are linked to stakeholder capitalism will be a very attractive proposition.

The wider world will be dominated by the environmental agenda and the mass introduction of artificial intelligence. Whole professions will disappear, just like the trades of old. Work will not return to the old 'normal' for millions. Attracting the best young workers of the future will require the promotion of quality products and services with an ethical and moral compass at their heart that synergies practicalities with ideals. Companies that respect, challenge and reward employees through progressive stakeholder capitalist business models such as employee ownership will, in return, win respect and quality contracts from customers. All businesses need to begin orienting to the next generation of workers, and it needs to start now, right at the beginning of the journey, a journey of change.

Pioneering the case for employee ownership.
There is a case, and a place, for pioneers of progression to champion and promote the benefits at a political leadership level to encourage an evolution amongst the next generation of workers, whom all of society will rely on.

Preparing for Change and Understanding the Bigger Picture

Change in ownership, whether it be from a trade sale or through an employee ownership model, is a significant decision from a business owner's perspective. The change, and specifically the transition to an employee ownership model, will result in a power shift. Despite the best efforts of a team of employees who have bought into the vision of this progressive model, the former business owner's role, even where a restructure has taken place, is vital for a short time to ensure continued success. Without a doubt, the founder will have been instrumental in setting the company's strategic direction and will have defined the mission and vision, and instilled the organisation's beliefs and values. Historic success has been built upon the founder's direction. Though a change in direction will ultimately occur where a business's people become its owners, reaffirming these core foundations is critical. For this to occur, based on experience, it is vital that the founder remains in the business for a short period to transfer their strategic knowledge post change in ownership to cultivate the continued flourishing of the company.

Following a variation in ownership, the founder will be considered the spiritual leader of the company - both internally and externally. For a business to continue to grow and thrive, the founder's role is to guide and ensure its people see the big picture. In a working environment, it is natural that human beings, by their very nature, are concerned with their own work and, by and large, will focus on their individual role. This could include a sole concern of their 'own' customer/s, without any serious consideration to the company's wider customer base. The paradigm of an individual employee only considering a specific area, whether it be a specific role or customer, has to change. For this to occur, the founder, though frustrated at this realisation, will be responsible for everyone in the organisation seeing the bigger picture, which relates to the sum of the parts. The collective value that a business's customers bring is an informative and mentoring process. A change in mindset is required, where all a business's people learn to appreciate the entire work and role of all an organisation's people. When this occurs, everyone will understand each and every role's value and fully appreciate that all customers contribute to an organisation's success.

A business's continued success is primarily concerned with customer satisfaction, which is directly linked to growth opportunities. It is more than likely that the founder has been the instrumental player in the growth of a business. This includes being the customer-facing leader of a company, responsible for attracting new business and setting the executive strategy to ensure successful delivery of the services provided. Following a change in business model, a company founder must have an exit plan. For this reason, it is absolutely necessary that other people in the business develop and learn new skills to have the ability to see, create and seize opportunities with new and existing customers. The founder's responsibility is to mentor and guide their employees into having the mindset and cognitive skills to take on this most important of leadership roles. It will not occur overnight, and the process will be fraught with frustration. However, what is guaranteed is that where the very best culture has been instilled, new leaders will emerge who understand the company and what it stands for. All employee-owned businesses will have people who fully embrace change and see personal opportunities for development and progression. These people, who unreservedly adore the culture and the underpinning foundations of the organisation that have been created, can take a business to new levels of success. These leaders will come from the next generation, and their mentoring post change in ownership is crucial for the organisation's lasting success. It will ensure a redesign in an organisation's culture that adapts the business and positions it for success in a post-COVID-19 world.

The bigger picture.
Employee ownership makes change inevitable. It cannot be a case of business as usual. The role of the company founder is critical; it has to encourage a wide understanding across the whole organisation of every role and work provided to all of their customers. Those leaders who will emerge from the next generation will require mentoring and involvement in senior management decisions. These leaders are those who will build on historic success and take the business to greater levels of success than those created by the founder.

From an external perspective, there is also a new role for the founder: being a pioneer of stakeholder capitalism and championing employee-owned business models. They must promote how EOTs can significantly encourage growth and success as the economy battles its way back to a position of strength following the COVID-19 pandemic. The pride associated with transitioning to an employee ownership model from a founder and seller's perspective to the people who become owners is unparalleled. Team motivation increases, along with the appetite for further business success and growth. These are stories to be told, where pioneers of employee ownership models can share and inform and play a pivotal part in the change that embraces tomorrow's world.

Applying the McKinsey 7S Framework to Implement Change

To support the management of change to an employee ownership business model, I applied the McKinsey 7S framework. The McKinsey 7S model was developed by Robert Waterman and Tom Peters in the 1980s and is used to analyse the internal operating environment. The model is based upon seven internal aspects. They are interdependent forces, categorised as hard elements (easy to define, management can directly influence them) and soft elements (less tangible and often influenced by culture). The hard elements are strategy, structure and systems, and the soft elements are superordinate goals (shared values), style (of management), staff and skills. The following model depicts how I applied the McKinsey framework. It shows that all internal forces are aligned and working together to ensure the change to employee ownership is successful.

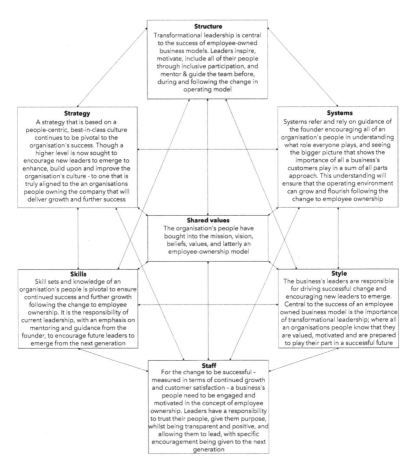

To summarise the seven aspects of the McKinsey 7S model as they relate to ensuring the success of change to an employee-owned business model, from experience, all aspects must be interconnected to:

- Build, maintain and continuously improve organisational culture through a strategy built on delivering a company mission and living by its vision, beliefs and values. These are core foundations in executing a change and transitioning to an employee-owned business model.
- Ensure management provide inspiration, motivation, inclusive participation, mentoring and guidance through the change.

- Maintain, enhance, build upon and improve organisational culture to drive growth and success.
- Ensure that all of an organisation's people understand everyone's role and the collective sum of the parts that all customers play in contributing to the business's success and growth.
- Encourage the next generation of leaders to emerge through transformational and participative leadership.
- Demonstrate that you trust your people, give them a sense of purpose whilst being transparent and positive.
- Provide appropriate training, guidance and mentoring to ensure that skill sets are maintained and continuously improved, as this will position a business for further growth and success.

In my experience, the McKinsey 7S model provides leadership with a framework that centralises the core values, allowing all other critical business success facets to work around and in harmony with what a business stands for. This extends to leadership and an organisational culture designed around delivering its mission and living by its vision, beliefs and values.

I have applied the framework throughout my managerial career, and it was the most important model from my toolbox of academic solutions when transitioning my company to an EOT. I used it to reinforce and align the business overriding the best-in-class organisational culture that has been my *Strategy*. I used the framework to define the following:

- Why and how the business is *Structured* the way it is.
- The *Systems* of communicating the bigger picture of the business to my employees.
- The leadership *Style* applied to inspire a best-in-class culture (my *strategy*), and drive change.
- Communicating the trust I have in my *Staff* to deliver the business's mission, vision, beliefs and *Shared* values.
- Ensuring that the business had the necessary *Skills* in delivering continued and future success and growth.

Working Towards Eleven o'clock
Establishing an EOT

Introduction

This penultimate chapter focuses on the mechanics associated with an Employee Ownership Trust (EOT) from the perspective of careful considerations, employee consultation, principles of an EOT company, what this type of business stands for, how it is governed, and how to get started with transitioning and changing from a traditional shareholder business model.

An EOT is an indirect form of employee ownership first introduced in 2014. An EOT can be an effective means of succession planning, with distinct tax advantages. For the seller/s, the sale of the company is free from capital gains tax and, for a company's employees, a yearly bonus of up to £3,600 can be paid, which is free from income tax. An EOT is a unique option for owners looking for an alternative way to pass on their business to its people and reduce their involvement in the business, either due to retirement, where an owner wants to move on and explore other opportunities, or to reward their employees.

An EOT business structure is becoming an increasingly popular exit route and has become a viable alternative to a management buyout or traditional trade sale. An EOT provides a solution for owners who are keen to protect their employees from the pitfalls that often come with ownership changes whilst rewarding them for their loyalty by allowing them indirectly to own the business they have helped to build.

The process, stages and steps involved in establishing an EOT are as follows:

- A new trust is created for the benefit of the company's employees. The trustees of the EOT will be a new corporate trustee company.
- A company valuation has to be prepared and agreed upon between the trustees and the selling shareholders. From an ethical perspective, a consideration for the seller should be to discount the value of a business by recognising the team's historical contribution and not burdening the trust company with debt.
- The corporate trustee company will then acquire between 51% and 100% of the company's shares, with a view to holding them for the long-term benefit of the employees. The consideration payable to the selling shareholders would typically comprise a cash payment on completion and an amount of deferred remuneration.
- As future profits are generated in the company, these can be paid to the EOT to make the deferred consideration payments to the selling shareholders.

Careful Consideration – A Focus on a Best-in-Class Culture

The last three decades have seen a gradual revolution in the ownership of many UK companies, with an increasing willingness among founders to involve their key employees as shareholders. Though offering a unique and distinct tax advantage for the owner/s selling the business, and employees who will receive a tax-free bonus (assuming the company is profitable), a company should not choose employee ownership only for tax reasons. It should be chosen because of an organisational culture where management and employees are already working together like a well-oiled machine and where values aligned to stakeholder capitalism are present.

EOT companies tend to have a positive culture and committed employees. However, employee ownership is not about creating a comfortable place. Like any business, they operate in a highly competitive environment and will only survive through financial success. Before considering or making the transition to an employee-owned business model, a company's organisational culture and leadership qualities must be assessed. Assessment, such as seeking Investors in People© accreditation, will either confirm that a business is in a good position to contemplate an employee-owned business model, or identify areas where improvements are required before seriously considering the transition. Where carefully structured and managed, employee ownership will support a business to achieve beyond historical levels and provide strong profits, sharing those rewards with everyone who has helped create its success. Being a part business owner does not make every employee a manager; like any successful company, one owned by employees will need a professional and effective management team. But its managers are far more likely to receive the support of employees committed to their company's success because they have a stake in the business and in delivering success and growth.

According to the Employee Ownership Association (2015), the UK's top 50 employee-owned companies now contributed over £20 billion annually and employed more than 150,000 people. It also reported that the number of employee-owned companies was growing at over 10% each year. Owing to historical management and staff engagement levels, employee ownership is unlikely to be suitable for every business, but there are many for which it will be. It is all dependent on having designed a strategy that is centralised around culture, strong leadership, a mindset that will allow for a successful transition, and a structure based on succession planning that will enable the next generation to develop into leadership roles.

Employee ownership must be carefully considered as it involves management having a demonstratable record of investing in communicating with employees to maximise their engagement. It revolves around management gaining the buy-in of all employees in delivering a company mission and living by its vision, beliefs and values. If a company has been built around a 'tell and do' culture, a transition to employee ownership will be difficult, if not impossible, as employees will be sceptical and cynical about change. Successful employee ownership relies on an existing culture of inclusive participation, where all employees feel valued, motivated, enjoy high levels of autonomy, and have the support of transformational leadership. By centralising culture as the key strategic driver from the company's creation, or well in advance of considering employee ownership, the transition will be easier. The business will already have foundations that will encourage employees to step up and for future leaders to be cultivated to ensure successful business leadership succession.

In establishing an EOT, arrangements should not be too complex; the simpler, the better. First and foremost, the design of an employee ownership structure should be built around what has made the business successful in the first place: a team that delivers the mission and lives by the vision, beliefs and values where organisational culture has been the key strategic driver of a business.

Ensure an EOT is right for a business.
Though an EOT presents distinct tax advantages for a seller/s and employees, ensure that these advantages do not obscure the decision in transitioning to an EOT. An EOT should be formed for the right reasons: an organisational culture that is led by the company mission, vision, beliefs and values, fairness, and equality, to further drive levels of success and growth, and to cultivate the next generation of leaders.

Consultation

The author would like to acknowledge Wrigley's Solicitors. This sub-chapter includes elements of information that Wrigley's provided prior to WAVE Refrigeration forming their EOT.

Understanding the mechanics associated with the workings of an EOT requires a significant amount of time. Seller/s, management and employees have a lot to absorb and learn about this business model. This section focuses on an overview of what employee ownership means, the principles of establishing an EOT, and the suggested content via a working party for employee consultation prior to the trust formation.

What Employee Ownership Means

Employee ownership is where all employees have a 'significant and meaningful' stake in a business. This means employees must have both:

- a financial stake in the business (e.g., by owning shares).
- a say in how it is run, known as 'employee engagement'.

Employees must have a say in how the business is run. Different ways of engaging employees are suitable for different businesses but can include:

- an employees' council, or another consultation group.
- a constitution that defines the company's values and its relationship with employees.
- employee directors on the board, with the same responsibilities as other directors.

The Principles of Establishing an EOT

A journey into employee ownership will pose three significant questions:

- What does this mean for employees?
- What are the roles of the company and its people?
- How do we ensure employees are properly engaged?

A redefined cultural journey begins as the company changes and the employees have rights and responsibilities. The eventual aim of an EOT should be 100% employee ownership. During the journey, it is important to understand what management and employees want to achieve throughout this transformation. Pertinent questions to be answered are:

- What should the vision for the future be?
- What do employees want it to include?
- What behaviours will help achieve that vision?

Structuring an EOT business model is critical. The following questions need to be answered:

- Who is going to lead on the employee ownership?
- How will the employee voice be constructively engaged?
- Are there any easy wins available on culture and engagement?

Regarding employee engagement, even in organisations that have centralised culture as its overriding strategy, the following questions have to be discussed and agreed upon:

- Work with the flow of the business. What happens now? What can be improved?
- There will be employee involvement in the EOT as one of the directors will come from the employees. How are they to be chosen?

The Role of the Trust

The EOT will be run through a newly incorporated company - the trustee - which will act as the legal holder of the shares in the business. The EOT will have rights as a shareholder set out in the Articles of Association of the business and through a Trust Deed, and it will have a role in promoting the company's success. An EOT will typically have three directors: one representing management, one representing the employees and one independent trustee director. Generally, the management representative will be selected by the seller/s. The employee representative will be voted into the position by way of an employee election, assuming there is more than one candidate. The independent trustee will be an external individual who should have a good understanding of business, management and people. Each director's usual terms of office are four years for a management director, two years for an employee director and three years for the independent director, though each may stand again. In the case of an employee trust director, this will be on a non-consecutive term basis. The EOT will be a company limited by guarantee, not shares, and each director will also be a member of the EOT. The guarantee is limited to £1.

Getting Started – The Formation of a Working Party

The management of a business transitioning to an EOT may or may not change as part of the process, and the current directors can remain in office.

It is essential for a working consultation party to be set up that consists of both management and employees whose role, facilitated by an external individual who will ideally become the independent trustee, will:

- Ensure the employees understand what employee ownership means for them and the company.
- Work towards an agreed timetable with all parties.
- Agree on the purchase price of the shares by the EOT (based upon the valuation being conducted, which they will also need to approve) and the period for payment; and
- Work through and agree on the various documents to be prepared to govern the companies once the EOT structure is in place.

During the working party phase, consultative workshops that discuss the legalities, role, governance and principles of an EOT need to occur.

The workshops should also be used to review an organisation's cultural position and seek to:

- Engage employees to drive better results post-restructure. The ownership of a business will shift from a traditional shareholder model to a model where all employees own part of the company, so they have a responsibility to drive future success and growth.
- Engage all generations to focus on approaches to best engage the four very different generations working side by side in today's workforce: Baby Boomers, Generation X, Millennials, and Generation Z. It is not enough just to know about the four generations present in our workforce today. It is time to truly understand them, which is crucial for business owners who form an EOT.
- Build higher levels of performance. Workshops should evaluate through existing measurement the current state of a leadership team, as well as the current state of employees. Then collaboratively build a plan to leverage strengths and eliminate weaknesses.
- Openly discuss the trap of unconscious bias. Everyone has their own biases, either consciously or subconsciously. These can have a profound impact on communication and decision making. Use the workshops to set the scene in communication expectations and how decisions are made in an EOT organisation to avoid the trap of unconscious bias.
- Focus on empathetic leadership. Empathetic leaders have the ability to maximise the engagement of their employees. Employee engagement is not linear: everyone has good and bad days, and engagement can often be predicted by what happens after the working day. While engagement is often seen as a top-down process driven by management, use the workshops to discuss and learn why successful businesses need to promote positive relationships between the business's leaders and employees. This is essential, especially for an EOT company to develop, grow and thrive.

- Learn how to have a difficult conversation. Whether it is verbally agreeing when someone does not agree, avoiding giving constructive feedback, refusing to hold people accountable, and/or dealing with difficult or different personality types. In EOT businesses, it is essential that difficult conversations are had when required. In any business, management will not be aware of all problems. In an EOT structure, everyone has a responsibility to either have or raise a concern where a difficult conversation is necessary.

The working party and consultative workshops will identify beyond doubt if a company is right or ready to become employee-owned. These sessions must be challenging, transparent and open. It is the one opportunity that employees who will be impacted by the change have to express any concerns they possess. This process, when run effectively, will bring to the surface any underlying issues within the business. It presents an opportunity to address any negativity, whether it be process-related or individual employee-related.

Applying Action Learning to Create a Culture of Continuous Change

From creating and growing my company to transitioning it to an employee-owned business structure, I have applied the Action Learning framework as a means of collective problem-solving. Whether one of process or technical in nature, when working together with a team to solve a problem, the resultant effect is an increase in learning, collaboration and thinking, whilst also building high levels of morale. The concept and application of 'Action Learning' as a management model, where used appropriately, can serve as a powerful tool for employee-owned organisations in collective problem-solving and decision-making.

The inception of 'Action Learning' originated in the work of Reg Revans in the 1940s when he held the post of director of education at the National Coal Board in the UK. Revans held the belief that managers who faced complex problems may benefit through increased learning by talking through such issues with one another. Johnson and Spicer (2010) state, "Revans thought that by sharing their concerns and plans with like-minded colleagues, the managers would gain greater insights, inspirations, and motivation to cope with difficult and challenging times."

A realisation of forming an employee-owned company is that Action Learning can contribute effectively to developing employees to think as owners and support organisational growth. Finding synergy with the foundations of Action Learning, Johnson and Spicer suggest that it is "an experienced-based approach to learning based on Revan's premise that managers learn most effectively with and from other managers whilst dealing with real world problems."

Though Action Learning would appear in nature to revolve around leadership, I have never considered the process restrictive in terms of who can and who cannot benefit from its framework.

The premise of Action Learning centres on a belief that formal instruction is not sufficient to achieve true learning. Revans introduced a formula to fulfil this achievement: $L = P + Q$.

Where:

- 'L' is the total learning.
- 'P' is considered knowledge provided by experts.
- 'Q' is regarded as insights from inquiry or powerful questions from the participants of the Action Learning set.

Based on the assumption that far too much emphasis is placed on the learning from 'P' and not enough on learning through 'Q', Action Learning advocates that challenges are seldom addressed through 'P' learning alone. Therefore, the role of questioning, or 'Q', is critical to the Action Learning process. Traditional education/training providers focus on teaching 'P' through experts, while people can teach 'Q' by focusing their inquiry on their own experiences that are central to the concept of Action Learning. The team's involvement in an employee-owned business would rely on their ability to contribute to 'Q', with the aim of meeting the requirements of 'L', essential for decision-making in an EOT to drive growth and success.

Johnson and Spicer introduced a case study of Action Learning in an MBA program in 2006, where their abstract identified:

A growing concern expressed by employers is the failure of universities to provide students with the skill sets needed by modern industry [...] it has been suggested that the learning afforded an individual by an MBA is of limited relevance to their current employer [...] Recognising this failing, universities are responding by developing new and innovative approaches to education. One such approach is the adoption and incorporation of action learning.

They go on to state that:

The MBA program considered here is, we believe, unique in being entirely centered on an action learning approach in which participants come together as a group to work on workplace-centered problems on an ongoing basis and gain an accredited MBA degree as a result.

Though the work of Johnson and Spicer is based on findings from an academic environment, a realisation is that Action Learning provides an innovative approach. Problems are considered on an ongoing basis and, as such, contribute effectively to real-world problems and, in the case of EOT organisations, contribute to collective decision making.

An Action Learning set would typically be made of six to ten people and follow certain characteristics:

- Investigate and act on real problems.
- Focus on individual problems as opposed to collective ones.
- Use questioning as a way to help Action Learning participants proceed with the problem.
- As a vital ingredient, include a group facilitator.

In the early days of forming an EOT, change is a central theme in understanding how employees learn to think as company owners. An EOT business, through regular workshops, will create various Action Learning sets, and, dependent on the specific theme, the facilitator will be the company founder, the employee trust representative, management, external trustee, or an employee.

There are four key elements in establishing a successful Action Learning process, and in the context of an EOT business, these are:

- How employees are engaged and contribute to the decision-making process.
- How employees learn to think as owners.
- How to cultivate employees to bring ideas forward to drive growth and success.
- A system for learning reflectively. In the context of driving the success and growth of an EOT organisation, this would be led by the Action Learning set facilitator.

A framework model of Action Learning that presents the process as an input-process-output model is introduced in the work of Johnson (2010). The model focuses on six components that Johnson includes as "an ethical standard for the practice of action learning". The following model depicts how I have applied Action Learning to cultivate employee engagement. This was to ensure the successful transition to an EOT company, and its continued success post-change from a traditional business operating model.

Action Learning Characteristics - as a Benefit to an EOT Organisation

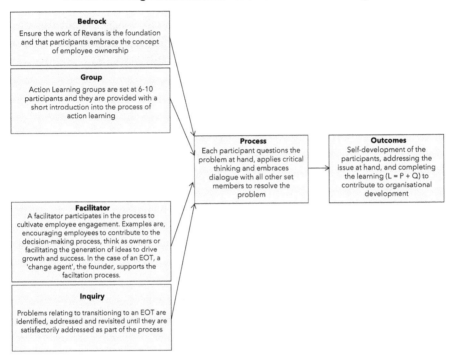

The outcome of the process should create and emphasise the implementation of ideas/solutions and subsequent individual reflections back to the EOT/employees. The result will allow Action Learning groups to be a continuous mechanism that will enable the company to grow and succeed. The transition to becoming an EOT is a significant change, and it is a model that has to be understood inside out by the facilitator/s. The success of an Action Learning set is dependent on the facilitator and the buy-in of all participants. In my experience of establishing an EOT, my role as a change agent, introduced in Chapter 8, helped support the transition once the change to employee ownership had taken place.

Since establishing WAVE, I have been the subconscious change agent, having spent six years developing a best-in-class culture. My role as a change agent has helped support and facilitate 'Change

Agency' among employees and management as the company transitioned, adapting to an employee-owned business model. The ability to facilitate an Action Learning group can be learnt. In the case of an employee-owned business model, this will enable the EOT to identify options for continuous and successful change.

Working Towards 12 o'clock
The End of the Beginning

Introduction

Chapter 12 is the final hour of Culture Redefined and represents one of personal reflection. It summarises my experiences of how stakeholder capitalism can present significant, fair and equitable opportunities through blending organisational culture with the progressive ideals of the Great Reset as the economy recovers from the COVID-19 pandemic.

From establishing WAVE, through its growth and culminating in an employee-owned business model, I remained steadfast. I centralised my team and organisational culture as the overriding business strategy whilst embracing a transformational leadership approach. The benefits in doing so have been the continuous engagement, participation and motivation of my team to deliver the business's mission and to live by the organisation's vision, beliefs and values. A best-in-class culture has seen the company win local and national awards and accreditations. These have raised the profile of WAVE, which has created new opportunities and allowed the business to grow. In designing a business strategy around its organisational culture, an environment has also been created that has allowed the next generation, the organisation's young people, to flourish and emerge as leaders of the future.

I have found that blending organisational culture with a transformational leadership approach has successfully allowed my business to introduce a continuous beyond-the-bottom-line programme of initiatives. My interpretation and implementation of the UN's Sustainable Development Goals were crucial in exploring and introducing the associated benefits of stakeholder capitalism through transitioning to an employee-owned business model. In creating an environment that thinks beyond traditional capitalism and centralising a company mission, vision, beliefs and values amongst its people, significant success can be achieved. I have first-hand experience of witnessing exponential growth in team morale and motivation as a result of introducing and achieving beyond-the-bottom-line goals.

Whilst beyond-the-bottom-line endeavours do not offer a tangible return, what they categorically do is add value through enhanced levels of engagement and teamwork, which inevitably carries over into the 'day job'. People want to work for businesses that care and are motivated to go the extra mile. Customers, both existing and potential, will be more likely to engage with a company that has a committed societal and environmental conscience. Activities that go beyond adding traditional value, such as supporting the Sustainable Development Goals, are the bedrock of stakeholder capitalism. In my experience, they can be taken to higher levels of success, supporting the overriding aim of the Great Reset and the change to an employee-owned business model.

It is the strategic design of an organisation's leadership and culture that are the key ingredients to move towards the progressive ideals of the stakeholder capitalist movement. Culture Redefined has taken the principles of stakeholder capitalism to a higher level by exploring, introducing and, in this chapter, demonstrating how employee ownership can take this leadership strategy and movement further. Although employee ownership may not be suitable for every business, from my experience of forming an EOT, there are remarkable synergies with both the stakeholder capitalist concept and the Great Reset.

The overriding principle of the Great Reset revolves around a commitment to build the foundations of our economic and social system jointly and urgently for a more fair, sustainable and resilient future. The reset also recommends a new social contract centred on human dignity, social justice, and where societal progress does not fall behind economic development. The global health crisis, exacerbated by the COVID-19 pandemic, has laid bare longstanding ruptures in our economies and societies and created a social crisis that urgently requires decent, meaningful jobs. Whether a renewed business strategy as a consequence of the pandemic is focused on stakeholder capitalism and/or employee ownership or not, what is clear is that both are aligned to the Great Reset. Either operating model presents an opportunity to build resilient businesses that are prepared for tomorrow's world.

Before steps are taken to align with stakeholder capitalism and/ or employee ownership, it is absolutely necessary to know and understand an organisation's position on leadership and culture. Its mission, vision, beliefs and values must be focused on goals that think beyond value creation for its shareholders. For this to occur, a business's focus should be centralised around its people. To ensure the survival and long-term success and growth of a company, a specific emphasis should be placed on developing its young people, the next generation.

The importance of Generation Z
It is Generation Z who will ultimately lead tomorrow's world. By setting up and cultivating a company focused on them, delivering a vision that goes beyond the traditional bottom line, and establishing an EOT, young people, under guidance and mentoring, will correct past mistakes and be fully engaged in the movement towards stakeholder capitalism.

For me, the WAVE EOT represents the end of the beginning. From a founder's perspective, the ethos and management of the business changed and began the transfer to its people. This is where the company truly commits to the stakeholder capitalist movement.

Transitioning from a Power Culture to a Task Culture

In creating, building and leading a successful people-orientated company, whilst operating in a traditional shareholder structure, a Power Culture as proposed by Handy is considered key to its success, where:

- Control radiates from the centre – people are encouraged to have absolute belief in their leaders.
- Power is concentrated among senior management.
- There are little in the way of rules or red tape. People are encouraged to deliver the company mission and live by its vision, beliefs and values.
- Decision making is swift – allowing people to be fleet of foot and work at pace.

The change to an EOT operating model is significant. Over time, a transition from a Power Culture is essential as a business's people are part-owners: they now contribute significantly to the destiny of the business. The focus and dynamic of the organisational culture have to transition, even if only subtly, to encourage collective decision-making. Task Culture, as proposed by Handy, can be considered key to the success of an EOT, where:

- Teams are formed to solve problems.
- Power is derived from expertise.
- There is no single power source.
- There is overlap between people and departments.

Action Learning and Communities of Practice (introduced later in this chapter) play a significant role in allowing the transition to a Power Culture.

Stakeholder Capitalism in Action

In the first six months of transitioning WAVE to an EOT business model, its turnover, when compared to the same six-month period the year before, is represented graphically below:

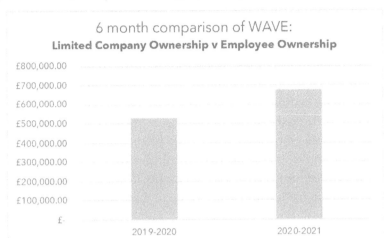

6 month comparison of WAVE:
Limited Company Ownership v Employee Ownership

The growth in turnover between the same six-month periods is in excess of 22%: profitability levels have been retained. The increase in turnover has largely contributed to enhanced employee engagement and motivation during introducing and establishing an EOT operating model and continuing to deliver the company mission, living by its vision, beliefs and values.

Remeasurement – Building Better

Following accreditation as Investors in People©, I began to plan what the future of WAVE should be and implement improvements. The mechanism I used was through the application of Deming's PDCA cycle. To encourage an environment of continuous improvement in leadership and culture, the following changes were made:

- A reinforcement of the company's mission, vision, beliefs and values.
- Providing a further focus on the business's beyond-the-bottom-line initiatives to ensure that people and the environment are aligned to the principles of stakeholder capitalism.

- Seeking new ways to inspire people with a focus on performance, communication, and feedback.
- Management agreed to an annual Investors in People© assessment to measure the quality of leadership and culture.
- Recognise and celebrate improvements made, then immediately identify and focus on further improvements to become better.
- During the establishment of the EOT, Action Learning principles were subconsciously introduced to the team. The outcome of the learning process fostered the implementation of ideas/solutions and subsequent individual reflections.

Though having already created an industry-leading culture, improvements were necessary to ensure that the change to an employee-owned business model would be successful. Following the transition, I organised and subsequently received our annual Investors in People© assessment, where we scored 866 out of 900. This demonstrated how the change in transitioning to an EOT company had further improved the leadership and culture at WAVE. The score represented an improvement of 32, representing an incredible uplift against the average Investors in People© benchmark score of 726 out of 900. The 2020 annual assessment ranked WAVE number 1 out of 155 small Investors in People© accredited businesses who operate in the construction sector and 38 out of all 1,917 accredited businesses (0-49 employees). In my opinion, the company is well placed for the future. This future is where all of its people hold a stake in the company, where greater levels of success will occur beyond those enjoyed under my ownership and leadership.

Our review identified improvements across the three Investors in People© indicators of Leading, Supporting and Improving. The tables below provide analysis between the original pre-employee-owned measurement (2019) and post-employee-owned remeasurement (2020) of pertinent 'strongly agreed' participant responses.

Leadership	2019	2020
The company develops great leaders	39%	86%
Communication of company's ambition	62%	93%
People believe that their managers motivate them to do their best	62%	93%
People believe behaviours which do not match the company values are challenged	31%	79%
People feel that they get the information they need to do their job	54%	79%

Supporting	2019	2020
People feel that they have had their performance discussed in the last six months	54%	86%
People feel that their manager helps them to improve their performance	62%	93%
People feel that they are consistently recognised for doing a good job	46%	79%
People feel that they feel appreciated for the work they do	54%	86%
People feel that they have the right level of responsibility to do their job effectively	62%	86%

Improving	2019	2020
People feel that the company invests in learning and development	77%	79%
People believe that they look for improvement ideas from their colleagues	31%	93%
The company has the ability to embrace change	39%	93%

In my opinion, the remeasurement through Investors in People© assessment identified three key findings:

- Leadership and organisational culture improved through taking learnings from our first assessment and introducing and applying Deming's PDCA cycle and Action Learning.
- The transition to an EOT business model has seen a high upswing in people who strongly agreed to questions related to leadership, supporting and improving.
- Identification that a stakeholder capitalist strategy can elevate success to higher levels, not only for WAVE, but any business that designs its leadership and culture around its mission, vision, beliefs and values.

In my opinion, stakeholder capitalism will secure the long-term future of any sustainable and ethical business and its people in a post-COVID-19 world.

A Former Business Owner's Role

Once I decided to establish an EOT, the biggest personal change was accepting that WAVE was no longer going to be my 'train set'. Having set about creating and implementing a people-centric culture, this change has been relatively simple to accept as my team are amongst the most motivated and engaged people that a business could hope to employ. The most significant and difficult acceptance was, and still is, a personal one. Like any business leader, I am not without my flaws, which relate to me being very passionate and needing to be the best. I wear my heart on my sleeve and demand nothing but excellence from my team. When I am frustrated, all of my employees know it. However, I have always commanded respect, as from my frustrations comes the ability to solve problems, be decisive, correct mistakes, build stronger relationships and ensure customer satisfaction. My flaws in many respects are what have made WAVE so successful.

My overriding concern for the future of the business was what happens when I leave, and this posed two questions, as it will for any business leader:

- Who is going to be the 'face' when I move on?
- Who else has the same level of drive and passion as me?

The answer to these questions is that no one can be replaced on a like-for-like basis, and, crucially, nobody is irreplaceable. Though I may outwardly possess high levels of enthusiasm and inspiration, this does not mean that other current and emerging business leaders care any less – far from it. All leaders are different, and, in many instances, it is those who are outwardly reserved who can achieve greater levels of success.

My concerns about the formation of an EOT eased on a week by week and month by month basis for three reasons:

- I have encouraged other people in the business to take on responsibilities that I had previously kept to myself.
- I devised an exit plan to place a sense of urgency on my departure. This included reducing my working week to four

days, which prompted the emergence of future leaders. From a former business owner's role, seeing this take place is highly rewarding!

- The realisation that the culture that I created will ensure the legacy of what WAVE stands for and will continue through my team, who are invested in its mission, vision, beliefs and values. It is a company that is truly aligned with stakeholder capitalism and the Great Reset.

If it were not for the strength of our organisational culture, I doubt that an EOT would have been possible. A lack of strong culture is what makes a trade sale an eventual outcome for many businesses. Irrespective of success or failure brought around by mergers and acquisitions, its people will only consider themselves to be workers who do a job. From forming the WAVE EOT until I depart, my role concentrates on mentoring the next generation, making suggestions, supporting decisions that are made by my colleagues, and the continuation of ensuring customer satisfaction. To ensure the lasting success of WAVE, I am actively encouraging the use and application of Action Learning through embracing stakeholder capitalism and, more recently, the concept of Communities of Practice. I encourage everyone to contribute to the generation of ideas, the direction and future of the business, and ultimately want my people to think beyond WAVE as a company that invests in them, but to think as business owners.

Transitioning to an employee-owned business model is simply the end of the beginning for WAVE. The establishment of an EOT sets the company on an exciting journey, where its people will now be responsible for the business's direction and success.

Communities of Practice

As introduced in Chapter 11, the concept of Action Learning presented a mechanism to generate ideas and solve problems that will benefit an EOT company to encourage growth and success. In the context of EOTs, Action Learning sets that are established to benefit employee-owned companies focus on an organisation's people, a team. Teams can be categorised as integrated units driven by goals that are generally defined and set by management. In the case of employee ownership, those people who are working within a set should, in my opinion, be categorised as members with a shared interest: the growth and success of the EOT.

Communities of Practice (CoP) are people who come together for a shared interest. They are members of a community and not actually a team by its classical definition. Wegner and Snyder (2000) define CoPs as "Groups of people informally bound together by shared expertise and a passion for a joint enterprise." A CoP is the essence of what an Action Learning set should be in the context of employee ownership. A belief of Habermas (1996) is one that I agree with: teams who deliver results often 'disperse afterwards'. In contrast, CoPs are held together for the long term and are driven by the value they provide to individual members: an overriding aim of EOT businesses. CoP members share insights, discover and generate ideas for the long term as they are bound together by their identity. In this case study, their common identity is the EOT. The following model depicts the delivery of Action Learning as a 'CoP' and as a 'Team' based on six characteristics.

Characteristic	Action Learning based on a "CoP"	Action Learning based on a "Team"
Is	What it 'Is': it is based on a theory of shared values bound together by a joint enterprise. There is little methodology, members share insights, discover and generate ideas based on their joint enterprise: the EOT	What it 'Is': it is based on a methodology that the team will solve a problem and produce a result defined by management and disperse on successful completion
Goal	What the 'Goal' is: a CoP encourages a knowledge domain, they discover value in diverse day-to-day exchanges of information and know-how. A CoP is a fellowship of individuals with a common goal: the success and growth of an EOT business	What the 'Goal' is: a team focusses on solving set problems. They are not necessarily defined by the shared values of a continuous joint enterprise
Participation	What 'Participation' is: it is based on varying levels of voluntary participation from the CoP members without set or defined roles. The aim is that members will provide insights based on shared information and goals in a fluid manner	What 'Participation' is: it is based on a fixed group who operate together over a fixed duration of time. There are clear boundaries and set roles within the team
Activities	What 'Activities' are: a CoP-based Action Learning set is based on learning activities of members that are based on joint enterprise. Learning is considered a communicative action through dialogue that exposes contradictions, doubts, dilemmas and possibilities	What 'Activities' are: a Team-based Action Learning set focusses on reflection and is considered the ability to make connections and develop and understanding of a situation
Expertise	What 'Expertise' is: it is considered as distributed expertise leadership from participation of all members	What 'Expertise' is: it is considered as peer-to-peer, based on the individual experiences of the team
Period	What 'Period' is: it is categorised as the life-stages of the CoP; in the context of an EOT this is a continuous journey as the business, grows and evolves	What 'Period' is: it is categorised as a determined period of time generally defined by solving a problem. An EOT is a continuous and evolving journey

For an EOT to be considered as a continuous and evolving journey, Action Learning sets of an organisation's people would be well placed to adopt a Communities of Practice approach. Participants are regarded as members who have shared values of a long-term joint enterprise: the EOT. An Action Learning set where participants are considered a team by classical definition could subconsciously affect the aims and success of the EOT due to the belief that teams disperse on completing and solving a problem.

Applying Johnson and Scholes Cultural Web to Drive Success

In establishing a business that designed its strategy around transformational leadership and creating an industry-leading culture, I always encouraged my employees to deliver our company mission and live by its vision, beliefs and values. I instilled a culture of ideas that think beyond-the-bottom-line, and, in doing so, growth and success followed. The culture of WAVE, where its people are continually striving to be better, raised the profile of the business that helped gain a solid reputation of achieving customer satisfaction and results. It also allowed for the successful change and transition to an employee-owned business model. For me, an EOT is a model that will promote and support a paradigm shift from capitalism to a fairer and more equitable future, where the world of business embraces the progressive ideals of stakeholder capitalism.

Since forming and growing WAVE, I have applied the work of Gerry Johnson and Kevan Scholes, who proposed The Cultural Web (1992). It provides an approach for looking at, changing and/or improving an organisation's culture. In my experience, the cultural web has been a key management tool and model that I have applied from formation, growth and transitioning WAVE into an employee-owned business. The Cultural Web has allowed me to design my strategy around organisational culture through correcting assumptions and practices and aligning key organisational elements with one another. The Cultural Web contains six interdependent elements that help to make up a central paradigm. Through assessing each element, a picture of organisational culture is created. It allows you to visualise what is working, what is not working, and what needs to be changed in your business's culture. Interpretation of the six elements and the paradigm are depicted in the following model:

I have applied The Cultural Web numerous times to look at the organisational culture as it is now, how I want it to be, and identify the differences between the two. These variations are the changes required to achieve a best-in-class culture. It is a concept that I have used and will continue to revisit throughout my career.

Final Reflections

A concern I had surrounding Culture Redefined is that early chapters may come across as patronising to some readers. This is not my intent. There are countless people who understand business management more than me. My aim of covering the topics in the way that I have is the hope that it may inspire people who will or have had to work hard from the bottom up to achieve ethical and sustainable success in the world of business.

In establishing, growing and transitioning my first company to the ownership of my employees, I have many positive memories and experiences to share. Based on my own experience, the importance of education and continuous learning in the world of business management cannot be underestimated. I hope that Culture Redefined conveys that practical leadership experience and academic theory are interconnected dependents. A common misconception and paradigm are that a practising manager or leader will not have, nor require, an academic background, but in my opinion, this is fundamentally incorrect. As someone who has been successful in business, Culture Redefined identifies the tangible benefits of possessing both practical experience and the ability to apply business management theory.

In the chapters, represented as hours progressed, working towards 12 o'clock, Culture Redefined introduces the societal and environmental benefits of stakeholder capitalism and employee ownership. Irrespective of personal opinion connected to employee ownership, it is unquestionably an operating model that has synergy with today's modern world, where people want more than just a job. People want to work for companies that focus on a people-centric culture as their key strategic driver. People also want to work for businesses where leaders believe and invest in them. They want to be part of organisations that care for the environment and aim to improve societal concerns with the same passion of achieving results and ensuring customer satisfaction. This is the essence of a redefined business culture.

It is the leaders of progressive organisations prepared to put their people first and those who embrace societal and environmental concerns whose companies will succeed in today's modern world. There is growing momentum towards a shift to stakeholder capitalism as society aims to 'Build Back Better' from the COVID-19 pandemic. A time for change is upon us!

References

Internet References

Authenticity Consulting. Action Learning (Peer Coaching Groups): Some Related Theories. Accessed April 18, 2021, from: http://www.authenticityconsulting.com/act-lrn/a-l/theory.htm

BBC (2021) Social Impact of WW2. Accessed March 4, 2021, from: https://www.bbc.co.uk/bitesize/guides/z6ctyrd/revision/6

Build Back Better (2021). Accessed March 12, 2021, from: https://www.buildbackbetteruk.org/

GOV.UK (2021) The ten point plan for a green industrial revolution. Accessed April 17, 2021, from: https://www.gov.uk/government/publications/the-ten-point-plan-for-a-green-industrial-revolution

The Guardian (2015) Is employee ownership right for your business? Accessed April 2, 2021, from: https://www.theguardian.com/small-business-network/2015/may/18/employee-ownership-business-john-lewis

Management Study Guide (2021) McKinsey 7S Change Model. Accessed March 15, 2021, from: https://www.managementstudyguide.com/mckinsey-7s-change-model.htm

Management Weekly (2020) McClelland's Theory of Motivation. Accessed February 26, 2021, from: https://managementweekly.org/mcclellands-theory-motivation/

St Scholastica College (2021) Lewin, Lippitt and Whites Leadership styles. Faculty CSS. Accessed February 27, 2021, from: http://faculty.css.edu/dswenson/web/LEAD/lippit&white.html

World Economic Forum (2021) Klaus Schwab. Accessed March 20, 2021, from: https://www.weforum.org/about/klaus-schwab

Business Management Textbook References

Burnes, B. (2004) Managing Change. 4th edition. London: Prentice Hall

Johnson, C (2010) A framework for the ethical practice of action learning. Action Learning: Research and Practice, Vol. 7 No. 3 pp. 267-283

Johnson, C. and Spicer, D (2006) A case study of action learning in an MBA program. Emerald, Education and Training Journal, Vol. 48 No. 1 pp. 39-54

Johnson, G. Wittington, R. Scholes, K. (2011) Exploring Strategy. 9th edition. London: Prentice Hall

McKenna, E. (2000) Business Psychology and Organisational Behaviour. 3rd edition. Sussex: Psychology Press Limited

Mintzberg, H. and Quinn J. (1992) The Strategy Process. London: Prentice Hall

Mullins, L. (2005) Management and Organisational Behaviours. 7th edition. London: Prentice Hall

Journal References

O'Donnell, D., Porter, G., McGuire D., Garavan, T.N., Heffernan, M. & Cleary P. (2003): Creating Intellectual Capital: A Habermasian Community of Practice (CoP) Introduction. Journal of European Industrial Training, Vol. 27, No. 2/3/4, p. 80 – 87

Wenger, E., & Snyder, W. M. (2000). Communities of practice: The organizational frontier. Harvard Business Review, 78, 139-145.

Acknowledgements

Culture Redefined would not have been possible without the team at WAVE Refrigeration. Specifically, I would like to thank the businesses directors Mark Williams and Alan Saban. I would also like to thank Sam Cameron, Ellie Clare and Gokul Divakaran, three former business trainees, who were my inspiration in writing Chapter 4, "The Next Generation". Gokul is one of four talented engineers who WAVE employ in India. On the 1st of July 2021, he became Vice-Curator for the Global Shapers hub in Trivandrum. Gokul will help lead the hub in taking an active role in confronting global societal and environmental challenges that young people have inherited. I am immensely proud of Gokul.

From establishing and growing WAVE, the entire team have embraced the organisational culture that I created. This has allowed the business to grow, thrive and become one of the most respected and successful organisations in the refrigeration industry.

I will be forever grateful to my friend and retired lecturer, Dr. Mark Joesbury, who has provided me with detailed and constructive comments throughout writing Culture Redefined. I have been fortunate to have been taught by some exceptional people, but, without a doubt, Mark was the very best.

A significant debt of gratitude also goes to my long-time friend from College Station, Texas, Randy Caperton, Pat Maughan of Daikin Industries and Kirsty Ford, for their valued input and comments.

I would also like to thank Investors in People© for endorsing Culture Redefined and for providing me with inspired guidance that has made WAVE Refrigeration one of the very best organisations to work for in the UK.

Finally, but most importantly, I would like to thank my family, particularly my wife Joanne, for her incredible levels of patience, support, and enthusiasm in making Culture Redefined a reality.

About the Author

James Bailey is a Chartered Engineer, Fellow of the Institute of Refrigeration, a Business Management Master's Degree Graduate, and in 2015 he set up his first company, WAVE Refrigeration. He has led his business in winning numerous local and national awards. He could be considered a stereotypical entrepreneur and advertisement for capitalism. He is neither. He was brought up in a northern working-class environment, where hard work, perseverance and determination were essential. Of all James' leadership traits, good, bad or indifferent, his biggest strengths are understanding people and listening. These traits have been instrumental in establishing, growing and leading WAVE Refrigeration in becoming an employee-owned company. Additionally, it is ranked as the number one of all small Investors in People© accredited companies in the UK's construction sector in December 2020.

Culture Redefined